Saying *Yes* to Change

Saying Yes to Change

Essential Wisdom for Your Journey

JOAN Z. BORYSENKO, Ph.D.,
and GORDON F. DVEIRIN, Ed.D.

HAY HOUSE, INC.
Carlsbad, California
London • Sydney • Johannesburg
Vancouver • Hong Kong

Published and distributed in the United States by: Hay House, Inc., P.O. Box 5100, Carlsbad, CA 92018-5100 • Phone: (760) 431-7695 or (800) 654-5126 • Fax: (760) 431-6948 or (800) 650-5115 • www.hayhouse.com • **Published and distributed in Australia by:** Hay House Australia Pty. Ltd., 18/36 Ralph St., Alexandria NSW 2015 • Phone: 612-9669-4299 • Fax: 612-9669-4144 • www.hayhouse.com.au • **Published and distributed in the United Kingdom by:** Hay House UK, Ltd. • Unit 62, Canalot Studios • 222 Kensal Rd., London W10 5BN • Phone: 44-20-8962-1230 • Fax: 44-20-8962-1239 • www.hayhouse.co.uk • **Published and distributed in the Republic of South Africa by:** Hay House SA (Pty), Ltd., P.O. Box 990, Witkoppen 2068 • Phone/Fax: 27-11-706-6612 • orders@psdprom.co.za • **Distributed in Canada by:** Raincoast • 9050 Shaughnessy St., Vancouver, B.C. V6P 6E5 • Phone: (604) 323-7100 • Fax: (604) 323-2600

Editorial supervision: Jill Kramer • *Design:* Charles McStravick

Library of Congress Control Number: 2005933233

ISBN 13: 978-1-4019-0778-4
ISBN 10: 1-4019-0778-5

09 08 07 06   4 3 2 1
1st printing, January 2006

Printed in the United States of America

To our children and grandchildren:

Justin, Regina, and Little Eddie;

Ben, Shala, and Emma;

Andrei and Nadia;

Natalia, Shawn, and Alex

Contents

A Parable

Once upon a time, the Angel of Death came to Earth to escort a saintly man back home to heaven. God, the Spirit of Love and Guidance, told the Angel to grant the saint any boon he chose, since he was a pure soul who had dedicated his life to compassion. The saint's most fervent wish was for God to retire the Angel of Death so that all people could live forever in a peaceful, predictable world without change.

As soon as his wish was granted, life on Earth came to a halt. Seeds, unable to die and shed their skins, could no longer release their vitality into new growth. White clouds hovered in a preternaturally still sky, their life-giving moisture denied to the parched earth, which baked in the sun of an undying day. The soft womb of night, from which life emerges new every morning, was driven into exile by a day without end. Eggs and sperm, deprived of the ecstatic merging that creates new life, languished in isolation. Soon the starving inhabitants of a changeless world became hollow-eyed and desperate, imprisoned in perpetual misery.

The saint's desire to make all beings happy by preventing death had unwittingly caused a holocaust of all that lives. As he watched the agony of changelessness unfolding before him, the wide-eyed saint became frantic with regret. He understood that attachment to what is, no matter how precious, precludes the possibility of surrendering to the freshness of creation. Knowing now that death was the mother of life, he begged for the Angel to be sent on his rounds once again.

The mysteries of change that the saint realized are known in every culture's wisdom tradition. It's those insights that will be brought alive for you in this book, so change can become a guide to your clearest, wisest, and most compassionate self.

How This *Book* Came to Be

by
Joan Borysenko

Writing a book is hard work. This is my 12th, and each one seems to be harder than the last. But this time there were special circumstances. My husband, Gordon, and I had given a seminar together on the wisdom of change and decided that it would be exciting to write about it together. We'd been married for all of two weeks when we naively sat down at our computers, fingers poised above our respective keyboards, prepared for a delightful, co-creative writing experience. The process was duly humbling, but the good news is that we're still married, and even planning a second book. But before you read any more of *this* one, we thought that it might be helpful for you to know a little bit about us, and about our writing process, so you'll identify more personally with our different voices in the text.

Gordon is an organization development consultant, sometimes known as a change agent. He gets called in to "stir the pot" and facilitate better communication when corporations get stuck in ruts or need a new vision. He's also been a student of the Ridhwan School, the "Diamond Approach" to self-realization, for more than 20 years.

I, on the other hand, am a psychologist, medical scientist, speaker, and writer who's been described as a Jewish, Buddhist, Hindu, Christian, Sufi, Native-American psychoneuroimmunologist. The author of 11 previous books and a monthly column called "Staying Centered" for *Prevention* magazine, I have my own very practical, personal, and slightly irreverent writing style. It's all I know, and while I'm not likely to win a Pulitzer Prize, I admit that I'm attached to what I know how to do.

Gordon, who was trained in literary criticism and the history of ideas, as well as in organization development, has a much more abstract, poetic style. In fact, reading his chapters out loud will give you a very different sense than reading them silently.

My husband's fount of information is enormous, and a simple thought is likely to land him (and you) in the depths of Dante's *Inferno,* the heights of T. S. Eliot's *Four Quartets,* or a commentary on how Theseus negotiated the labyrinth. When people asked us how the book was coming along as we were writing, I often replied, "Imagine Peanuts meets Kierkegaard." Gordon's fear was that the book would be too superficial; mine was that it would be too deep and abstruse. Our mutual hope is that it's authentic and true.

As you read along, you'll notice that the chapters are written in three different voices: Mine, which will be noted by the initials **JB**; Gordon's, which will be prefaced by **GD**; and ours, which won't have any initials attached to it at all. We decided on this framework because it preserves our distinct styles and also the unique sensitivities that two genders can provide.

Gordon's worst moments were when I tried to edit his pieces and changed his voice to a feminine one, while mine were when neither of us could seem to find our voice at all. In spite of (or perhaps because of) the ordeal, writing this book really was a transformational experience. It taught us about partnership as we struggled to find an authentic "we" without losing our individual sense of autonomy. In conceiving each chapter together, and discussing every point in detail, we both learned an enormous amount. For that, we're grateful to Hay House for giving us this opportunity—and to you for placing enough trust in us to read what we've written.

Introduction

Two Kinds of Stories

The caption underneath one of our favorite cartoons from *The New Yorker* reads: "A man about to meet his destiny." It shows a guy happily walking down the street with clear visibility of what lies ahead . . . yet around the next corner, a gigantic rhinoceros is galloping toward the intersection, where the two of them will unexpectedly collide in just a moment's time.

Life is like that. Throughout our brief time on Earth, we all face change in countless ways. Some events have the earthshaking quality of meetings with destiny, while others are more in the natural order of things (but still difficult). We humans are creatures of habit, secure in what's familiar, and change—at least the unwanted kind—is almost universally feared. Even transitions that we desperately need are often hard to make; consequently, most of us have had the experience of staying too long in situations that are draining.

Saying yes to change, as the title of this book suggests, is an invitation to faith—not the kind that rests on doctrine—but that which is rooted in trusting our own inner experiences as they unfold. In that process, our true nobility, our essence as compassionate and wise human beings, gradually emerges.

Transformation is a promise of change that repeats itself in stories from every era. The young prince Siddhartha leaves his luxurious palace to become a wandering beggar and fulfills his destiny as Buddha. Christopher Reeve falls from his horse and becomes a quadriplegic, but instead of choosing depression, he says yes to life. His equanimity, compassion, and desire to help others make him into a real Superman.

We go to inspiring movies, read books, and contemplate the reasons for existence because we want to be transformed, too. And although few of us would choose to meet our destiny like Reeve did, it's often unsettling change that's the truest teacher. The stories that spawn chills of recognition and inspire us with the hope that we can transcend our suffering are the ones where the balance of power shifts away from outside events that "happen" to our inner style of questioning, reflecting, and interpreting those events in a new way.

Inner stories don't generally get much play in our world of shallow "action figures" where reflection appears strangely out of place—in other words, we tend to prefer Rambo to Hamlet. In 1992, Ross Perot's running mate, the decorated war hero Vice Admiral James B. Stockdale, seemed oddly kooky when he introduced himself at a televised debate with the most spiritual of questions: "Who am I, and why am I here?" If *he* didn't know, the viewing audience seemed to snicker, why should we vote for him? But this was how he chose to begin telling his story.

The stories we tell ourselves about major life transitions are extremely revealing. There are essentially two contrasting ways to recount our experiences. One chronicles *externally focused* striving: where we're going, what we hope to do when we get there, and the frustrations we meet along the way. The other kind is *internally focused*. It describes who we're becoming, the interior ascent into the realm of being, and our journey toward the discovery of what's most meaningful and precious. It often includes engagement with that ancient wisdom question that Stockdale invoked.

Externally focused stories are linear: They move along the horizontal line of chronological time, from past to present to future, which is the normal plane of human experience. Internally focused stories, on the other hand, begin with endings, then transcend clock time *(chronos)* altogether. They break through into an entirely new dimension *(kairos),* where clock time is suspended in favor of eternal presence, the timeless realm of the here-and-now. That's when apparent miracles happen: Synchronicities guide us, unexpected allies appear, and the linear world is punctured by a new and powerful reality that's a force for guidance.

Because change is a transition during which we move from what was to what will be, from the known world of chronos to the nonlinear world of kairos, it's akin to an initiatory rite of passage. In this book, we'll focus on inquiries into essential questions that emerge during the different stages of the classic three-part rite of passage that mythologist Joseph Campbell termed the Hero's Journey. Curious, open engagement with the questions that arise when things fall apart—or we break them apart—is the essence of courage and self-discovery. It's a path to transformation that requires no dogma, just a commitment to being authentically present to what's happening in your own experience.

The CD included with *Saying Yes to Change* contains a meditation exercise designed to help you focus on the present moment as it unfolds. Practicing with it once a day will also help calm you down so that your inner wisdom can emerge. The other practice you'll find in here is called *inquiry*. Most of the chapters are organized around one or more essential questions for you to inquire into in terms of your own experience, and this invitation to self-reflection is the heart of this book.

Reading something and acquiring knowledge as an abstract principle is very different from embodying a subject and knowing it deeply in terms of your own experience. To that end, an invitation to participate in the experiential dimension is included at the end of each chapter in a section called *Reader's Reflection*. We've included space for you to write down your thoughts on the essential wisdom questions posed at the end of each chapter, so you can review your insights and add to them at any time. (If you need more space, we suggest that you use a journal dedicated entirely to reflecting on the change process.) Whenever you're in transition, you can review the previous insights you made and apply them in order to help guide you in your current situation.

Saying yes to change isn't ultimately about digesting someone else's wisdom . . . it's about finding your own.

Most of the chapters concern the wisdom of transition—that time after your old story has ended but before the new one has begun. Wandering through the wilderness of change is a pathless journey, and only you can find your way. The topics we chose to include apply to a wide range of transitional situations, from grieving serious losses to understanding courage, and most of them stand alone and can be read in any order. We hope, by virtue of this organization, that this book will remain a valuable guide in the future as your situation alters and different topics become more pressing.

And with that, let's now learn how to *say yes to change*.

Chapter 1

The Natural Intelligence That *Guides* Transformation

JB: My doctoral thesis was about biological transformation and how the hidden intelligence inside each cell communicates with the whole entity as change is happening. I netted a tank full of tadpoles from a local pond and then studied them at intervals as they metamorphosed slowly into frogs. The same question that guided my research then is still exciting now: *What is the natural intelligence that guides transformation?*

Tadpoles are fascinating to watch. They're orderly change artists, masters of subtle and sneaky transformation. Perfectly engineered water wonders, tadpoles have big heads and graceful, tapering tails that offer little resistance to forward movement. With no fanfare at all, the pollywog simply starts to change one day: His tail gets shorter as his body absorbs it, and he sprouts four tiny limb buds.

Day by day, powerful rear legs and delicate forelegs take shape, a sculpture in progress. Seemingly oblivious to the stunning internal and external remodeling, the tadpole continues to swim, eat, and rest until he becomes an amphibious masterpiece capable of living both in the water and in the air. From the human perspective at least, this elegant process occurs organically and gradually without undue fuss or bother.

Caterpillars metamorphose into butterflies in a much more startling way. One day the caterpillar suddenly finds herself spinning a chrysalis—one minute she's crawling around munching leaves and the next she's hanging from a thread, imprisoned in a silk coffin. Unlike a tadpole, she doesn't just grow new body parts that allow her to move effortlessly from earth to sky. Instead, new cells called *imaginal cells* begin to multiply inside her. Then her immune system goes into hyperdrive, desperate to destroy the would-be invaders. The caterpillar's imaginal cells multiply and overwhelm her immune system; in fact, the poor little being actually liquefies, while her imaginal cells feed on caterpillar soup. Triumphant, they finally gather into a community, differentiate, and form an entirely new creature: the phantasmagorical winged beauty called a butterfly.

The caterpillar had the seeds of transformation, the imaginal cells, within her all along. But she had to die completely to her old life to be born into the new form that was her true nature, essence, and destiny. Perhaps we're similar to our winged sisters in that there are seeds of essential humanity embedded within us that grow and evolve in the wake of life-shattering crisis and change.

All in all, I'd rather transform like a tadpole, but no one ever asked my opinion. As I look back over 60 years of life, it's easier to see big caterpillar-like meltdowns such as divorces, betrayals, and the deeply distressing death of my younger son's best friend in a car crash when he was barely 17. It's harder to notice the small tadpole-like transformations that include becoming more patient, appreciative, or discerning.

The great American philosopher William James, the founder of modern psychology, once noted that human beings transform both through sudden *crisis* and slow *lysis* (a process of disintegration or dissolution). A central question that interests me about both processes is what enlivens them. After all, we generally don't choose to have crises, and we aren't even aware of lysis as it gradually helps us shed an old skin. If these kinds of changes aren't consciously initiated, where do they come from? Are they sparked by something akin to the plant hormone *auxin* that causes the stem to bend toward the light, or is there a deeper mystery still? Where is the ghost in the machine?

We've all watched clumps of grass and impressively hardy weeds pop up through tiny cracks in concrete walkways . . . there's a will to thrive that all living things share, from tiny one-celled organisms to human beings. Every species has its own genius for overcoming obstacles and aiming at the perfection of its form. "The force that through the green fuse drives the flower," Welsh poet Dylan Thomas's famous line, seems to apply just as well to the evolution of human beings as it does to plants. There's something that urges us on to our full potential until we, too, come to flower and then cast seeds of reproduction.

I'm reminded of when my friend and colleague Jean Houston, truly a master of human potential, was interviewed by psychologist Jeffrey Mishlove on his remarkable Public Television series, *Thinking Allowed*, which aired until 2002. Jean told a story of being befriended by the extraordinary French Jesuit, paleontologist, and philosopher Pierre Teilhard de Chardin. She'd literally run into him in Central Park when she was 14 years old; following their collision, the two became friends.

Of her walks with de Chardin, Jean explained, "It was extraordinary. Everything was sentient; everything was full of life. He looked at you as kind of a cluttered house that hid the Holy One—and you felt yourself looked at as if you were God in hiding, and you felt yourself so charged and greened with evolutionary possibilities."

When I've listened to Jean speak, she's often talked about the "Godseed" within us. Using her metaphor, change splits the shell of that seed and allows us to fill the form of the Holy One that we're destined to grow into, just as an acorn is destined to become an oak. That's a great philosophy, one that makes me sigh with satisfaction and belonging as I read it. But its test, of course, is in the living, not the metaphor. I want to know what being the Holy One (or at least a wave in the great ocean of that One) might look and feel like for me. And I want to know how it might be different for you. I'm less interested in generalities than a truthful dialogue about what it means to any of us to become our real selves, our unique God selves.

The term *Holy One,* of course, means different things to different people. A noted priest I admire recently participated in a Christian/Buddhist dialogue in Boulder, Colorado, followed by a Jewish/Christian dialogue in Denver. He sidestepped the childhood version of the "Guy in the Sky" with a beard and a black book quite deftly, and by the end of the dialogues, it was clear that he and both of his audiences were all speaking about the same thing (although the Buddhists omitted the word *God*). They all spoke of a consciousness, or a "Ground of Being," inherent in every person. The nature of that consciousness—whether you call it "God," "the Great Mystery," "Yahweh," or like the Jewish mystics "the Ein Sof" (the endless endless)—is wisdom and compassion. That's the secret energy, the natural intelligence that both does the work of transforming us and is the nature of transformation itself.

Reader's Reflection

Can you remember a time when the world as you knew it fell apart and you were transformed in the process? What did this feel like? How do you perceive the world differently now? If you can't remember a personal story, think or write about a powerful account of change that happened to someone else, even if it was in a book or a movie.

assassination of JFK ; Martin Luther King
September 11, 2001; Ralph moving out;
my mother's stroke: It felt like
I had no control over my life,
it felt like there was no handbook
for what to do next. It felt like
life was very unfair. And now I
try to be grateful for what is —
whether I think I wanted it, or not.

Chapter 2

Rites of Passage

"Tomorrow, and tomorrow, and tomorrow creeps in this petty pace from day to day . . . and all our yesterdays have lighted fools the way to dusty death." That's Macbeth's bare-bones description of the straight line of cause and effect, wear and tear, which seems to be "a tale told by an idiot, full of sound and fury, signifying nothing." It's a monotonously repetitive and meaningless view of the story of our lives. You walk the plank, and at the end you fall off into the sea. Whether you've been good or bad, heroic or cowardly, doesn't matter—the end is the end.

So where in this story, or any other, does change allow a breakthrough to transformation? And what is transformation anyway?

A friend of Joan's, Jim Curtan, had done an exciting interpretation of the film *Cast Away,* starring Tom Hanks, at a course that she'd attended, so we decided to watch it together from the perspective of transformation. *Cast Away* is not only the story of an unexpected catastrophic change, but it's also a truly elegant demonstration of the three-part process that's been described by anthropologists as a rite of passage from one stage of life to another.

Hanks's character, Chuck Noland, is a hard-driving, clock-watching FedEx systems engineer who metaphorically worships Chronos, the God of Time. *Tick, tick, tick* goes his mind, and nothing is more important than shaving a few minutes off of worldwide delivery times. The relational aspect of Noland's life is a pale specter in comparison to his endless work as a harried road warrior. There's no time for the woman he loves, he wolfs his food down on the run, and he can't even look his colleague—whose wife is dying of cancer—in the eye. He's not a bad guy, just a preoccupied, unconscious one.

Noland's old life ends abruptly when the FedEx plane carrying him to Malaysia crashes in the South Pacific, and he's the only survivor. Marooned on a desert island for four years, he's sustained by the antique pocket watch his fiancée gave him for Christmas on the night they parted. The mechanism is ruined when the plane crashes and time stops—both literally and figuratively.

Chronos has, in fact, become irrelevant in the new dimension Noland has entered. It's the picture of his lost love, mounted in the top half of the watch, that keeps him alive. Several packages wash ashore with him, and one contains the other source of his salvation: a soccer ball. Noland paints a face on it with the blood of his wounded hand and names it Wilson (the brand name on the ball). It's this imaginary friend who becomes integral to Noland's developing compassion.

Chuck Noland's four-year sojourn in the ocean wilderness is a time of transition. His old life went down with the plane, yet he hasn't yet been reborn to a new one. He's in a kind of no-man's-land, a transitional place where there's plenty of time to think about the meaning of life. The end of his long evolution from the man he was to the man he's becoming nears an end when the carcass of the plane's restroom finally washes ashore—he's able to build a raft and use the metal structure as a sail. The ordeal at sea on the tiny vessel is terrifying, and the defining moment comes when Wilson washes overboard in the aftermath of a storm.

Torn between swimming out to sea to rescue his friend and staying with the raft to save his own life, Noland chooses survival. His grief is almost unbearable, a tribute to the humanity that's been growing inside him during his ordeal on the island. But then magic happens: A whale keeps watch over him, singing mysterious songs of beauty; and in the nick of time, a ship passes by and rescues Noland.

The Chuck Noland who returns to America, however, is a far different man from the one who left. Just after his rescue, he's able to look straight into the eyes of the man whose wife was dying when he left, and with deep humanity, Noland apologizes that he wasn't there for his friend. He's become a *mensch:* a wise and compassionate human being. His fiancée, meanwhile, believing him dead, has married and had a child. Their reunion is poignant, and while it's clear that she'd give up her marriage to be with him again, he knows that she's found a new life that needs to be honored.

Cast Away ends with a reflective, mature Noland standing at the intersection of four dusty country roads, the same place where the film began. It's a deeply symbolic image, as it's both a crossroads and a cross itself. Father Thomas Keating, a modern Christian contemplative, speaks of the cross as symbolic of two movements in our lives. Its horizontal arm represents the death of our time-bound false self, or the ego that developed early in life to keep us safe by conforming to other people's notions of what it means to be "human." The vertical arm represents resurrection into the realm of kairos, the eternal present in which our true nature resides.

Moving from one to the other—from the fearful, time-bound world of chronos to the compassionate, timeless world of kairos—is at the heart of the transformational journey. But what does this mean in practice? That is, how does the shift from one story to another happen? Well, sometimes in life, particularly when the rug has been pulled out from under us and we can't rely on our old ways of thinking and acting to keep us safe and happy, we have an insight. Something clicks.

King Lear, for example, was ridiculously trying to hold on to his royal privilege and inflated sense of power despite the fact that he was over-the-hill and everyone knew it. He just didn't get that the king story was over. Finally, humbled to nakedness by the events of his life, his true nobility emerged. The character at the center of one of Shakespeare's greatest tragedies had a realization—there was a click, a recognition that "I am a very foolish, fond old man."

At that moment, an astounding transformation occurred: The shell that Lear had formerly presented to the world as his identity dropped away and shattered. From it emerged the pearl, the luminous dignity, of his undisguised being. Lear became vulnerable and human—the person he really was when he gave up trying to play a role. That's the secret of transformation: The person we're becoming is none other than who we really are.

The Three-Part Journey

In rite-of-passage stories, the protagonist recognizes and embodies his real self in a three-part journey. First, he or she is forced to leave the known world and all that's been loved—and the loss and separation are wrenching and irrevocable. Perhaps you've had that experience: Maybe you lost your job, had to declare bankruptcy, or had a health challenge. When a person is diagnosed with cancer or AIDS, for example, they often say that it feels like the earth just opened up and swallowed them. Nothing is the same as it was just a moment before—they've died to the person they were, yet they haven't yet been reborn as who they will someday become. That sudden catapulting from the known into the mystery is the end of the first stage of the transformative process.

In the second phase of the journey, the protagonist enters a transitional state, what Cornell anthropologist Victor Turner (who studied ritual in the Ndembu tribe of Southwest Zambia) called *the liminal phase*. The initiate stands at the *limen,* or the threshold of something new, but he hasn't arrived at transformation yet. For instance, the boy who leaves his mother's hut to go into the forest for circumcision is no longer a boy, but he's not yet a man either. This intermediate stage is a place of magic where chaos rules, and even the usual constraints of thermodynamics may be overcome.

The Belgian-American scientist Ilya Prigogine won the 1977 Nobel Prize in Chemistry for his theory of "dissipative structures," which opened up a new understanding of the value of chaos. In essence, he posited chaos as an evolutionary force, in which the breakdown of old systems can lead to unexpected, nonlinear breakthroughs when they "escape to a higher order" of complexity. The chaotic, transitional phase of the change journey is often marked by such unusual types of breakthroughs. It's as if the very fabric of time and space are becoming torn apart, allowing unexpected events to occur.

Synchronicities abound in the transition phase of change, and healing and insight are frequently marked by surprising occurrences that seem to come out of left field. New people may arrive and become allies on the journey, and wisdom can and does appear in archetypal, and even seemingly magical, forms. The whale that accompanies Chuck Noland through the end of his liminal phase on the raft at sea in *Cast Away* is a non-ordinary ally, typical of the kind of grace that often appears during intense chaos.

Getting through the chaotic, transitional period of liminality in traditional rites of passage involves facing numerous ordeals: Noland has to cross the sea on a flimsy raft; Jason has to slay dragons to get the Golden Fleece in the Greek myth; and Snow White has to be poisoned and go into a state of apparent death before love awakens her. One of the most remarkable aspects of these obstacles is that they can't be faced and overcome in the usual linear manner of the chronos world. The initiate must become still and give up his personal will to attune with the higher wisdom of kairos. This is a challenge in its own right because it's contrary to the usual way that the ego functions, using personal will to push forward. The transitional period when we stand at the threshold of possibility crackles with both danger and opportunity. The danger is getting so stressed out that anxiety, depression, and despondency take over; the opportunity is self-realization.

The third stage of the rite of passage is return. The Ndembu boy who left his mother's hut in the first phase of his journey usually spends a year or two in the bush becoming a man. In his transitional period he learns from other men what it means to be a warrior and a man of heart. And he also spends time alone learning to know himself (just like Chuck Noland did). The person who finally returns from the initiation is not the same person who left. The boy has become a man with authentic wisdom to give to his tribe—the journeyer, having found true strength, offers it to the community for the common good.

Joseph Campbell called the three-part transformational sequence of self-realization "the Hero's Journey." Hollywood films often use it as a storyline because there's an innate understanding in each of us that we're watching the greatest story ever told: the soul's true journey home. Framing the stories of change in our own lives as rites of passage, such Heroes' Journeys give us a way to see through and grow beyond surface appearances that are often so discouraging.

There's a Buddhist saying that states that at the beginning of the journey to one's true nature, mountains are mountains and rivers are rivers. In the middle of the journey, mountains are no longer mountains and rivers are no longer rivers. And at the end of the journey, mountains are mountains again and rivers are rivers. And T. S. Eliot expressed the paradoxical ordinariness of the extraordinary transformative experience beautifully in "Little Gidding," the fourth of his famous *Four Quartets:* ". . . and the end of all our exploring will be to arrive where we started and know the place for the first time."

· ● ● ● ·

Reader's Reflection

If you're in a change process, where in the three-part rite of passage are you right now? Have you experienced synchronicities in the liminal stage? How, while in this phase of transition, can you come to the required stillness so that needed insights can more easily come through to you? And finally, what would change be like if you saw it as an initiation to wholeness, a transformation to your true nature?

Chapter 3

Inquiry
as a
Path
to Freedom

JB: Inquiry is the process of facing the facts of life with both eyes open. It's the antidote to the illusion of knowing, the key competence for traversing the unknown territory of change and making new discoveries. Kids are naturally curious, inquiring into everything—this reflects a strong instinct to fathom reality, to see beyond the surface aspects of life into its depths. Queries such as "Where do the hummingbirds go in the winter?" or "Why do clouds move?" arise from a deep desire to relate to the unseen mysteries of the natural world.

However, "Why is Daddy mad at you?" "What's wrong with ninth graders having sex?" or "Why is there terrorism?" are much more complex. Here, the child is learning about emotional literacy, interpersonal sensitivity, politics, history, and morality. She's engaged in the process of forming conscious, intricate interrelationships with an expanding, multilevel world. Questions like "What happens when we die?" and "Is there a God?" are existential inquiries geared at coming into a more intimate relationship with the universe at large.

But as we get older, most of us stop questioning so much. We've formed our opinions—and we often go to the grave with them, even though we may not have ever really thought them through. Maybe we just downloaded them from our parents, teachers, or the television; but when we go to open them up through inquiry, they're like empty icons on the computer with nothing in the file.

I grew up as a Jew in an Irish Catholic part of town. One day two boys chased me home from school, throwing rocks and yelling, "Get out of here, you dirty Jew!" I yelled back, asking in the literal way that kids do, what was dirty about me. "I don't know," one boy snarled, "but my father says so."

Opinions are powerful motivators and separators. If your view of a certain ethnic group is negative, you may attack them like the boys did me. Or maybe you'll just stay away from them and never learn to see who they really are. Yet when we separate ourselves, the loss is always ours. Without intimacy and openness, there can be no evolution, and the result is that we remain in our smallest selves. One of the basic facts of life is that we experience our larger, more authentic selves by coming into real relationship with others.

Inquiry, at its heart, is a way of coming into right relationship. If the boys who'd chased me had been older (and willing), perhaps they could have contemplated the question *Why do I hate Jews?* If their parents or priests called Jews "Christ killers," but the boys were able to look a little deeper, they might then have asked, "But did that little girl kill Christ?" After a few more questions like this, the absurdity of hating an entire group of people—and an unknown person—might have become obvious. When the artificial boundary between "them" and "us" disappeared, those boys might have discovered a rich relationship to a whole new dimension of life that had been entirely outside their experience.

Why Me? An Inquiry on Why Bad Things Happen to Good People

Change is a fertile time for meaningful inquiry, and that's why it has the capacity to set us free. The most common question asked during tragedy or unwanted change is "Why me?" That's a fruitful inquiry, because it brings beliefs about our place in the universe out into the open. But here's an even deeper question that cuts through the self-centeredness and superficial thinking of the ego: "Why *not* me? Is there something that makes me so different from all the other people in the world that I think I should be immune to impermanence and suffering?"

From the beginning of time, human beings have short-circuited the inquiry process through guilt. If something bad happens, the thought that we did something wrong to deserve our fate gives us the illusion of control. If we'd acted or thought differently, the logic goes, we might have experienced a different outcome. So if we just think or act perfectly, then by definition we'll lead a charmed life. We don't like the fact that bad things sometimes happen to good people for no apparent reason—it's easier to think that they (or we) did something to deserve it.

This kind of fearful thinking is the root of both new-age guilt and old-age *religious* guilt. In the first instance, people blame themselves for thinking wrong; in the second, individuals believe that they've offended God and are being punished for their sins. Neither position is likely to hold up to inquiry. After all, if you've ever read the Old Testament story of Job, who loses everything, then you know that his friends sit with him and question why things fell apart so badly. They want to believe that he did something to deserve it, but Job knows that he's blameless. That's almost impossible for his friends to accept, since it means that none of us have control over tragedy. It can happen to anyone.

My mother, for example, lost her faith in the "He'll make everything all right" God of childhood when the Holocaust took place. Everything was *not* all right, and the very worst kind of suffering was inflicted on innocent people. Her response to the horror was to denounce God and stomp away like an angry child. Perhaps she asked questions about God that I didn't know about, but what I did hear from her was a strong belief that there couldn't be a God in a world where suffering was nonsensical.

Guidelines to Individual Inquiry

When you're ready to look at your assumptions about why bad things happen to good people—or any other question—there are a few guidelines that can make the process more insightful. First, try writing your reflections down, either in this book or in a journal. Don't edit them or worry about sounding good—you're making an inquiry into what's true, not trying to please someone. After you've written down everything that comes to mind, ask yourself those tough questions again. Keep writing, and more insights will come. When you're finished, try questioning your beliefs a third time.

Throughout the exercise, stay aware of the sensations in your body. Emotions are the interface between body and mind, and the emotional response to your thoughts is a strong indication of their meaning. Perhaps you're writing something like, "What am I feeling about why this is happening to me?" and when you sense your body, it's tense and restless. As you contemplate those feelings, you realize that you're angry—now you're getting below the surface. Next, inquire into the anger. Follow the thread of what you're feeling, and it will lead you to the truth. At the heart of inquiry is the simple question: "What keeps me feeling separate from my experience or from other people, and what would happen if I could break through this barrier?"

Shared Inquiry

I was a postdoc at Harvard, and I walked past my professor on the way to my office. He didn't greet me—he didn't even glance at me—and there was a tense, hostile look on his face. I took it personally, sure that he was angry with me. I went into my office and sat by myself, feeling rejected and anxious. Then my boss's technician came in. She saw that I was upset, so I told her that Dr. X didn't say hello. She proceeded to ask me the obvious question: "Why don't you go to his office and ask him what's up? It probably has nothing to do with you at all."

Quivering with trepidation, I crept up to his door like a mouse and finally knocked. When he opened it, he was still glaring. But I stated my truth anyway: "Hi, Dr. X. This morning I passed you in the hall, and you seemed angry. I hope I didn't do something wrong. Is there anything we need to talk about?"

He looked up, suddenly smiling, and said something like, "You took that personally? I'm sorry, Joan—I was just preoccupied with my grant renewal, mentally reviewing the data. There's something in them that just doesn't make sense."

We spent the next hour together, poring over data and trading theories. The result was that I was thrilled to be treated like a colleague. Where there was separation between me and my professor, the most ordinary investigation of the truth created intimacy and allowed both of us to drop our masks and come into our true selves—and creativity flourished. This is an example of an *interpersonal* or shared form of inquiry, rather than an individual, *introspective* one. But in either case, the passionate desire to delve beneath appearances and discover the underlying truth makes inquiry an essential practice for liberation.

· • ● • ·

Reader's Reflection

Sensing your body (the enclosed CD will help you understand what sensing consists of), look into what you're feeling right now. Then take special care to reflect on this: "Why do bad things happen to good people?"

_____

_____

_____

_____

_____

_____

_____

_____

Chapter 4

The Three *Faces* of Wisdom

JB: I was sitting on the floor at a weekend retreat, listening with rapt attention to four elders (all over the age of 70) share their life wisdom with the group. They were responding to the question, "Looking back over your lives, what's the most important insight you can share with us?"

Christine, a thin woman in her 80s, looked around and smiled. She was clearly delighted by the group's interest in her experience, reveling in the chance to be heard and received. She pulled herself up straight and spoke slowly and with great dignity. "All weekend I've been hearing so many of you talk about being in transition and how hard that is," she said. "But when you get to my age, you'll realize that you're always in transition. The idea that life is stable, reliable, and neatly packaged is an illusion.

"Everything changes, like it or not. The only thing you can do is live in the moment with appreciation because before you know it, whatever you took for granted will slip away. Don't take that personally. It happens to everyone— bad things *and* good things happen—and don't bother trying to convince yourself that you're any exception to that rule. It's just a fact of life. Anyway, it's not so much what happens *out there* that's the measure of your life. It's what happens *in here* that makes all the difference," she finished, touching her finely veined hand to her heart.

Believe it or not, there are people who are actually wisdom researchers. They study elders like Christine to understand what wisdom is and how we can best acquire it. What we gain as we adapt to life's changes is like champagne that's been pressed from the fruit of adversity. Research tells us that wisdom has three identifiable faces: (1) right thinking; (2) self-reflection;

and (3) emotional intelligence. As you make your way through the chapters that follow, you'll recognize these three aspects of wisdom in your own experiences.

Right Thinking: On Change and Impermanence

The right-thinking aspect of wisdom involves coming to peace with the basic facts of life . . . and change is certainly one of them. One of the perks of where Gordon and I live in the Rocky Mountains is that the reality of impermanence is obvious: One minute it's sunny, and an hour later it's snowing. But *everything* in life is impermanent. That's often hard to remember, even as life moves by in a flash and things change with great rapidity. Right thinking tells us that there's no point grasping onto anything because there's really nothing to hold onto.

We humans don't like change; it makes us anxious. We'd prefer everything to stay the same—secure and stable. But accepting impermanence and transition are central to becoming wise. Understanding the inherent uncertainties of life, questioning and making meaning, accepting shades of gray, and developing the willingness to understand situations from multiple perspectives are the hallmarks of wise thinking.

Self-Reflection

Wise thinking alone isn't enough to make a wise *person*. Without self-reflection—the ability to see your behavioral patterns and learn from them—you're doomed to living your life like the movie *Groundhog Day*. In this brilliant comedy, which is truly a spiritual teaching, Phil Connors relives the worst day of his life over and over again in a seemingly endless loop. Phil, a self-absorbed weatherman, finally has a profound awakening when he discovers that, just as with the weather, everything changes . . . while at the same time, nothing really does. Once he realizes that the only authentic change that can ever happen is within himself, he discovers his own compassionate essence. At that point, Phil escapes from the endless repetition of the same story into wisdom that allows freedom of choice.

My mother was always eager to point out my own special Groundhog Days. When I'd break up with one beau, only to choose another who was similar (the SGDD, or "same guy, different day," syndrome), my mother would put her hands on her hips and sputter, "Book smart, Joanie. You're book smart. But look here, Miss Smarty Pants, if you don't start learning from your experiences, you're going to have a very unhappy life."

Subtlety was not one of her great virtues, but Mom was nevertheless pointing out the importance of self-reflection. If we can take a curious perspective and ask questions about how we've gotten into the situation in which we find ourselves, we're likely to do better in the future. It took years of reflection for me to realize that I kept choosing the same kind of man because of an unconscious program. You see, I loved my father, who tended to be melancholy, and tried throughout childhood to comfort him. So it felt perfectly natural to choose depressed or troubled men and then try to rescue them later in life.

Unfortunately, old patterns block growth and inhibit transformation because they're like running in place. Self-reflection is the only antidote to unconscious repetition. It's the practice of self-awareness that encourages the ability to perceive reality without distortions, projections, or self-centeredness. You can think of it as waking up.

Emotional Intelligence

The third face of wisdom is what researchers call *affective,* or rooted in feeling, and it involves emotional intelligence: the ability to feel, name, and act on emotions in a way that's healthy and creative. Emotional intelligence grows gradually out of practicing self-reflection and right thinking. Let's say, for example, that you don't get along with your boss and you're afraid of being fired. As you inquire into the situation, tracing your anger back to its roots, you recognize a pattern: You've never gotten along with *any* of your bosses. Authority figures automatically remind you of your father, who was belittling and judgmental—and you realize that the anger you've been feeling toward your manager is a carryover from childhood, and that old resentment has muddied the present situation.

Once you realize where your emotions are coming from, you can choose to behave in a different way. Instead of blaming the boss, you take responsibility for what you feel, and begin to create a present that's different from your past— that's transformation. The shift from blaming other people for your problems to taking responsibility for your own life is one of the most important gifts of change. And keep in

mind that periodic troubles are not the exception but the rule in human life. Because troubled times bring up emotional reactions, they have great potential in terms of developing emotional intelligence—as long as you're willing to maintain the stance of open, honest inquiry.

With time, emotional intelligence helps you become more real and transparent—anchored in the present instead of the past. The quality of openheartedness, genuine interest in others, and curiosity that characterize emotional intelligence is what Christine was talking about when she pointed to her heart and told the group that the real measure of life isn't what happens out there but what happens "in here."

Cultivating what's in here (one's essential or true nature) is a practice. Change is a fruitful time for that practice because it naturally invites the wisdom of self-reflection, especially when inquiry becomes central to the process.

· • ● ● ·

Reader's Reflection

Can you think of a repeating pattern that's caused difficulty in your life? What's your experience of it, and how do you account for it? What benefits do you gain from keeping this old pattern in place? What are some of the barriers to letting it go? What are the resources you have, or might find, to help you with this process?

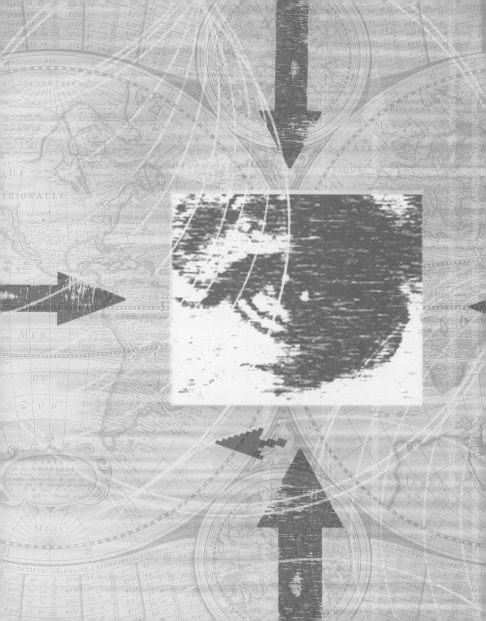

Chapter 5

Coyote Wisdom:

Seeing the *World* with New Eyes

JB: The Coyote, or Trickster, is a beloved character in many American Indian tribal cultures. He represents an archetypal energy that allows us to break free of stereotypes and see things that we're normally blind to. The Trickster is the master of crazy wisdom—illogical, funny, and unpredictable. It's said that he's the best teacher for lessons that we don't know we need to learn, and that once we've tasted his teachings we won't ever forget them. The Coyote is a study in opposites: He's at once cunning and stupid, creative and destructive, selfish and unwittingly generous. He's wily, lusty, and quite down-to-earth. And while he's often represented as a clown who helps us find the wisdom in our folly, he's also a penetrating energy who aids us in seeing things as they really are, rather than as we believe them to be.

While the Trickster is a staple of folklore and teaching stories in both Africa and North America, many people don't know how to recognize or work with his energies. This chapter is a very humble introduction to the instinctual Coyote Wisdom that exists in every one of us, and that guides us in our journey of transformation. Unlike the other three kinds of wisdom (which we covered in the last chapter) that are conscious and self-aware, Coyote Wisdom is unconscious. It works through unexpected and unplanned events that break the trance of everyday assumptions.

Whenever you experience synchronicity, for example, the Trickster is at work revealing patterns and delivering wisdom that your conscious mind isn't always capable of apprehending. We'll start with a literal story about a local neighborhood coyote, and then move on to the metaphoric way that this powerful energy shows itself, particularly during times of transition, which are natural opportunities to learn how to see the world with new eyes.

Living at 8,600 feet in the front range of the Rocky Mountains, it's not unusual to see coyotes or to hear them singing, ghost-like and haunting in the moonlight. But one afternoon Gordon came home with a strange and compelling tale. He was driving down the long dirt road that leads into our tiny town when he saw a coyote standing right in his path, blocking the way. It caught his eye and held it, an extremely provocative and unusual move. We wondered what the animal might have been trying to communicate, but nothing immediately came to mind. At the very least, the encounter was mysterious and unsettling and left both my husband and me feeling slightly wary.

Two hours later I was at my computer when I smelled smoke. Through a combination of unusual circumstances (including a heavy snow that temporarily occluded the vent pipe), our trusty 35-year-old boiler had morphed into a flaming dragon that ignited the dry plywood floor underneath it. In the previous week the pilot light had blown out twice, but instead of inspecting the furnace carefully, Gordon and I had just relit it. Fourteen firefighters, all neighbors from our volunteer fire department, responded to the blaze with great skill and speed. Thankfully, the flames were put out before too much damage was done, but the "coyote coincidence" stuck in our minds. Was the coyote my husband had seen trying to warn us to pay attention? Did the fire itself have a message for us? We wondered what else might blow up if we failed to notice the early warning signs of malfunction.

When people write about the Coyote as humorous, that's only one of his faces. The fire wasn't funny at all—but it *was* thought-provoking, as well as an occasion for deep appreciation. Both Gordon and I felt unexpectedly blessed by the near disaster. Had we been out, some of the firefighters assured us, the house would almost surely have burned to the ground. What a wonderful grace that we were home when it started, and how precious our home seemed in the light of nearly losing it.

I'd lived in that place for more than ten years before I even met Gordon, and I always describe it as a cross between a ski lodge and a cathedral. It's a funky old mountain house with lots of stained glass and some real potential. Gordon and I spent the first two years of our relationship restoring it and making it our home, our nest, a field of love that we hoped would also nurture seeds of creativity and service. But I admit to feeling some ambivalence about it.

The house is situated in one of the most beautiful spots on earth, with a breathtaking view of 70 miles. But it's also cold up here, and when spring comes to Boulder—a mere 20 minutes down the mountain—we're still starring in reruns of *Nanook of the North.* Some spring days we're up to our knees in mud, and Sasquatch, our little white Maltese, comes home from walks looking like a 100-year-old egg. That's when I fantasize about moving down the mountain and leaving dirt roads and muddy driveways riddled with puddles far, far behind. I can't appreciate the beauty that's here because I'm too busy resisting the climate and wishing I were someplace else.

I realized that the fire was an invitation to break that old pattern of complaint and come into a deeper relationship with these magic mountains, seeing our home for the magnificent place it is in every season, rather than resisting it for what it isn't.

Coyote Wisdom Opens Up Our Eyes

Coyote Wisdom is a reminder that *creation is based on relation* and that when judgment supersedes curiosity, the creative dance of life stops. Our false self becomes the boss, the know-it-all whose menu of experience bears no more relation to reality than a map does to the people who live in each town. One of the Trickster's primary teachings is that all forms of resistance are an opportunity to come into right relationship with whatever we're resisting.

Coyote Wisdom was easy enough for us to recognize when the actual animal stepped out in front of Gordon's car, leaving his calling card for future reference. But how can *you* recognize the invitation to look beneath the surface of things, and to see beyond your blind spots and judgments, when the Trickster's energy is working through other channels? The key is to notice highly unusual or synchronistic events, which are definitely out of the usual flow.

Here's an example of how the Coyote pointed out a blind spot of mine through a series of unusual synchronicities that came during a period of unwanted change, which I wrote about in my journal.

> I'm upset about a colleague who was untruthful and has done substantial damage to my business. With news of his betrayal, my world has tilted slightly on its axis. The trust I had in him is shattered, and I wonder about myself as well. I'm full of questions: Is this my fault? What signals did I miss? How could I have let something like this happen? I'm obsessing, rerunning the same thoughts over and over, and no new wisdom is emerging.
>
> Kathleen [who works in our office] understands that I'm stuck, preoccupied, trapped in my mind, and not at all

present. I have an appointment in Boulder, and she's worried about how I'll manage to get there all in one piece. She gives me a hug and warns me to pay attention to the road and drive super carefully. I back the car into the same turnaround in our driveway that I've used thousands of times before. But I come too close to a tree and shear off the side-view mirror. There's the Trickster: He'll do anything to get your attention, particularly unusual things. If he could speak he might have said, "Joan, you're blind as a bat. You've lost your perspective on what trust is and you can hardly see a foot in front of your face. You've fallen asleep, hypnotized by your judgments and beliefs, so heads-up here—I'm going to offer you a teaching."

I go back into the house, ignoring the Coyote's message, and continue to stew in resentment about the betrayal. A few weeks later, the day before a weeklong trip to a conference center in the Caribbean, I'm minding my own business, cruising slowly down Canyon Boulevard in downtown Boulder. The light turns red, and I stop. All of a sudden a city bus comes up on my left, and as it turns—would you believe it?—it cuts too close and rips off my brand-new mirror.

I can't believe it. Forty-some years of driving, and I've never lost a side-view mirror. Why now? Why two? I still don't want to think about it—there are errands to do and a suitcase waiting to be packed. But if you don't get the message, the Trickster won't leave you alone with his synchronicities. I go on the trip, and a man I've never met before sits down next to me at lunch. Out of the blue, he tells me a story of betrayal by a colleague that exactly mirrors my own. The next day a woman sits down next to me, and without any cues, launches into another story that mirrors my own. Those coyotes are relentless when they're on your trail.

I give up, go to the beach, and sit quietly. It's time to ask the basic Coyote Wisdom question: What am I resisting, refusing to come into right relationship with? My mind keeps going back to something that both the man and the woman have said: "It's not our fault that these betrayals happened—we're just trusting people."

A mental bell rings. [My administrative assistant] Luzie often tells me that I'm an innocent. It's suddenly clear what she means—I've never figured out what trust is. I review my current definition of the term, which is that anyone who looks sincere must be. But assuming that everybody is always operating with your best interests in mind isn't trusting at all. It's stupid. Something clicks—the old pattern is disrupted, and I know clearly that trust isn't something you gift someone with, like a dozen roses. It develops organically from the relationship, growing mutually over time as agreements are honored. *Trust*, clearly, is a verb rather than a noun.

Before the trip, I'd been poised to make the same mistake again in another relationship. But the Coyote trotted to the rescue. Finally—two side-view mirrors and two messages from strangers later—he got me to toss out an old concept that made me blind to what was really happening. This time I didn't repeat my pattern and make the same mistake. Instead, I waited for authentic trust to develop between that person and me before we made business agreements that had the capacity to affect the course of my life.

One of the dangers of change is the very human desire to re-create what we've just lost, racing through the liminal period and the uncomfortable time of uncertainty that characterizes it. But the liminal stage is the Trickster's true home, and disrupting old patterns that don't serve us is part of his role. He's most comfortable on the edge, at the margins, in the in-between places. His wisdom is most potent during transitional times, in the mysterious unknown, the holy parenthesis between the old and the new.

Transformation requires us to see clearly, rather than continue in confusion or resistance. Coyote Wisdom thrives during chaos, when we become more willing to enter into authentic relationship with what is, overcoming old forms of resistance. That's the Trickster's gift.

Reader's Reflection

Write about a time when you saw through a blind spot and came into right relationship with something that had previously been a lifeless belief. Have there been times in your life of synchronicity, of meaningful coincidence? What significant changes occurred at that time? Can you think of an instance when the Coyote came into your life, upset your usual sense of things, and shocked you into paying attention to something new or meaningful that you'd overlooked?

_____

_____

_____

_____

_____

_____

_____

Chapter 6

Who's to Blame?

When change disrupts the usual flow of life, we typically do one of two things: blame ourselves or blame forces outside ourselves. Either response is a diversion from what the situation is really calling us to do, which is to trust ourselves and to pay close attention. The importance of paying attention is what Edgar Allan Poe illustrates in his short story *A Descent into the Maelström*.

When the narrator's ship is caught in the whirling vortex of the maelstrom, breaking apart and about to be swallowed by the sea, he has the presence of mind to notice that some of the debris is positioned in the current in such a way that it goes with the flow. He watches as it's momentarily sucked down to the bottom and then is ejected back out to safety beyond the maelstrom's reach. Now he knows how to position himself. Such presence of mind—that is, the ability not to fear, blame, or try to explain, but to pay attention to what's actually happening—is what the unsettling movement of change calls for.

We can inquire much more meaningfully into what's really happening if we understand what psychologists call *attribution theory*. What comes up automatically for us when something is upsetting? What do we attribute it to? And how can we let go and yield to the flow of guidance that's always right there, beneath our usual way of responding to things?

JB: My father made a bold choice to die with dignity when his medical treatment for leukemia produced a manic state that ruined his—and our family's—quality of life. Waiting until my mother fell asleep one night, he silently sneaked into the living room of their high-rise Miami condo, opened a window, and jumped to his death. In the weeks (and years) that followed, my mother tormented herself with the thought that she was to blame. If only she'd been up at 3 a.m., she reasoned, then perhaps the moment for his choice might have passed, and he would have lived.

So many times we sat together—she, filled with survivor's guilt, needing to tell her story over and over again, as she sought some atonement for a sin that consisted simply of being alive while her dearest love was dead. Not knowing any better, I tried to talk her out of her feelings. I'd tell her that Dad's death wasn't her fault, which was totally obvious to anyone. But survivor's guilt isn't rational—it's not a healthy guilt that provides feedback on our behavior by telling us that we've missed the mark. Rather, it's a wish for what's not possible: omnipotence.

As children, omnipotence is a natural feeling. If a parent dies, a child may believe that she's responsible because she wished them dead one day when she was angry. That's part of why loss is particularly hard for children, particularly if they don't get the opportunity to talk about their fear and guilt. As adults, when we lose someone or something we love, it's natural to regress emotionally. The childhood feelings of omnipotence sneak up in the form of irrational survivor's guilt.

My mother's response to the guilt—at least the part of that response that was obvious to outsiders—was to punish herself. Perhaps if she were never to be happy again, that would be penance enough for her imagined transgression. She stopped calling friends and locked herself away in her apartment for the 13 years she remained alive. But even self-imposed solitary confinement wasn't enough to banish the horror of surviving her lost love.

With time, Mom finally did stop talking about Dad's death. In contrast, it took me years to even *begin* to talk about it or start the grieving process. I often wonder if I could have been a better listener, or whether in my own pain I just cut my mother off until she stopped trying to speak about it. Being emotionally unavailable to her was part of my own survivor's guilt.

Talking things through over and over again comforts and connects, but it also helps the brain rewire trauma. Traumatic memories are stored in a part of the brain called the *amygdala* in the form of icons or images. The amygdala is part of the limbic system, which processes emotions, so when anything triggers images of the loss, we instantly feel the pain again. Talking helps transfer the memories out of the powerful icons in the amygdala into a part of the brain called the *hippocampus,* which stores information in words. As the hippocampal circuits get stronger, emotions quiet down, and the thinking mind can bring a larger perspective to the loss. That doesn't make the loss any less real, just less painful.

Buddha compared pain to a cup of a salt: If we pour it into a bowl of water, that water will be bitter and undrinkable. But if we pour it into a lake, the water will still taste sweet. In other words, talking through trauma over and over again—and being received by people who love and respect you—can be the neurophysiological equivalent of taking the salt out of the bowl and pouring it into a lake. The pain's still there, but we're able to become more spacious around it. Gradually, rather than taking up most of our mental space, it takes up a smaller and smaller part of it. That's especially true when we're willing to open up space in our outer life to do new and meaningful things. Getting outside yourself by focusing on what you can do for others creates a much larger lake for the pain to dissolve in.

We've thought about why some people never recover from trauma, while others undergo startling and inspiring transformations. Some of the difference has to do with attitude, and what we attribute the trauma to in the first place. University of Pennsylvania professor Dr. Martin Seligman is a master of attribution theory. Whenever something goes wrong, he's found that pessimists typically blame themselves—that is, they attribute the problem to their own shortcomings. Furthermore, they generalize beyond the immediate situation—not only do they believe that they're at fault for their current problem, but they also think that they generally mess up everything they do and that this unfortunate pattern will continue until the day they die.

Seligman calls these unshakable attributions the "Three P's": Pessimists blame themselves and take things *personally;* they think that their bad fortune is *pervasive* throughout their life experience; and they believe that this sad pattern is *permanent,* the story of their lives.

Optimists have an entirely different attribution style, and our hypothesis is that they recover from survivor's guilt more easily than pessimists because of it. Psychologists Suzanne Kobasa and Salvatore Maddi studied the way in which more optimistic people think about change in a landmark study of AT&T executives. At the time, the company was undergoing reorganization, which was stressful and filled employees with uncertainty—not only were their job descriptions changing, thereby creating confusion, but they realized that soon they might not have jobs at all.

The study compared executives who thrived and maintained good physical and mental health to those who got stressed out and fell apart. The stress-hardy executives shared three characteristics that Kobasa and Maddi called the "Three C's." The first C stands for *challenge*—the hardy executives were a realistic group who understood that change is an inevitable and important part of life. Instead of a threat to the status quo, they thought of transition as a chance to develop new strengths. High self-esteem and a sense of empowerment led them to assess new circumstances as an opportunity for growth and mastery.

The second C stands for *commitment*, which is a measure of meaning. If your life has deep meaning, you're hardier than if you think of it as a meaningless exercise in survival. The third C is about *control*. Stress-hardy executives didn't waste time trying to mold what was out of their sphere of influence. Instead, they focused on what they *could* do to improve their circumstances. Even if you have no control over whether you have a job tomorrow, for instance, you can still control the quality of your work today or what you eat and whether you exercise.

JB: I'm a pessimist by nature. When something bad happens, my first response is to blame myself and then to shame myself. That leads to unhealthy guilt, which—for better or for worse—is built into my brain circuits. Over the years, I've learned to notice my attributions and realize that my pessimistic thinking isn't the Truth with a capital T—it's just a thought pattern. That insight allows more spaciousness, the chance to back up and take a wider perspective, to pour the cup of salt into a larger body of water.

Knowing that it's possible to think differently, I like to imagine how a stress-hardy person might think in my place. If I'm scared about losing something, I try to think about what strength the situation is challenging me to develop instead. That's the first C: Is this change a threat or an opportunity? If I feel out of control, the question becomes, "What can I realistically control right now?" That's the second C. Perhaps the most important shift is in frame of reference— the third C—what we're most committed to. Over the years,

I've developed a commitment to bravery and courage, a growing—if halting—willingness to stay with the experience as it unfolds. And that's the seed of transformation.

Even if you're a pessimist by nature and don't call up the Three C's automatically, you can certainly learn to imagine doing so. That's the beginning of freedom, and it's why psychologists like to study what they call *competencies*. If you know how a competent salesperson thinks and acts, for example, you can teach other people their secrets—that's sales wisdom.

Learning to think in a stress-hardy way is *change* wisdom that can help you avoid the pitfall of self-blame, minimize the paralyzing effects of guilt, and hold a framework for transformation rather than desperation.

· ● ● ● ·

Reader's Reflection

Think of a time when some unpleasant change happened in your life. What did you attribute it to? Use the framework of Seligman's Three P's to determine whether you were thinking like a pessimist, and Kobasa and Maddi's Three C's to see if you were thinking in a more stress-hardy mode. Be specific about your attributions by carefully reconstructing what you might have said to yourself.

What Doesn't Destroy Us *Makes* Us Stronger

The Boston Red Sox winning the World Series in 2004—with almost magical panache—was a special thrill because they finally overcame the famous "Curse of the Bambino." The team's string of outrageously bad luck began in 1920 when its owner sold Babe Ruth's contract to the New York Yankees to raise money to produce his girlfriend's play. You've got to hand it to the chronically luckless team and their fans, though: They didn't give up hope and lose their spirits, even after the seemingly insurmountable ordeal of a losing streak that went on for more than 80 years. They hung in there.

JB: As a former Bostonian from a long line of Red Sox fans, I believe that my home team honed their special genius against the barren bone of adversity, finally rising victorious like a phoenix from its ashes. As the 19th-century philosopher Friedrich Nietzsche famously noted, "What does not destroy me, makes me stronger."

Life's ordeals can either divert us from transformation or facilitate the discovery of new strengths. There's a whole genre of wisdom literature, for example, that's been written in prison. For example, during the Middle Ages the most popular book in Europe, next to the Bible, was *The Consolation of Philosophy,* written by the imprisoned Boethius. Modern prison wisdom includes books like *Soul on Ice* by Eldridge Cleaver, and *Soledad Brother* by the African-American activist George Jackson.

At age 17, Jackson was accused of stealing $71 from a gas station. Clearly innocent, he was nonetheless sentenced to "one year to life" in the Soledad Prison in Salinas, California. He never made parole, and seven and a half of his first ten years were spent in solitary confinement. But rather than breaking, as many people would have, Jackson transformed himself into a preeminent revolutionary scholar and champion of prison reform in a system that routinely abused black men and overlooked them for parole. After being unjustly accused of killing a white prison guard, he was murdered, yet his life had deep meaning.

Nelson Mandela had a very different experience with his prison guards, whom he came to treat with great respect, thus blurring the distinction between friend and enemy. Eventually, they returned his respect, and Mandela, who invited the guard closest to him to his inauguration when he became President, demonstrated how forgiveness and compassion can bridge impossible distances.

One of the reasons why children enjoy fables and fairy tales is that they often have a motif of succeeding against all odds. Since the stories we hear as children become part of the fabric of our wisdom, we'd like to present two of our favorite stories about overcoming obstacles with you here. Perhaps you'll share them with the little people in your own life, and when they meet with challenges later on, they'll remember the wisdom teachings you left with them.

JB: My favorite tale about faith and perseverance concerns a frog who falls into a bucket of cream. The sides are slippery, and he can't find anywhere to rest his legs, so he's trapped. But he's a brave little frog and does the only thing available that affirms life: He swims, even though there's no apparent hope of salvation. He swims because it's not in his nature to give up. After hours of paddling in circles, the frog is finally exhausted and on the brink of death. At that very moment his rear legs touch something solid, and with a mighty leap he jumps out of the bucket to safety. All the swimming finally churned the cream into butter.

GD: As a child, I read a similar kind of story about a boy my age, and I've been inspired by it ever since. Set in medieval times, the father of the boy in the story brought him to the local castle to apply for a job as a page. If he could succeed in that role, the child could advance to squire and then ultimately become a knight. To his father's great delight, the boy was accepted as a page.

One day he was walking along one of the castle's ramparts when he passed a deep hole in the stone pavement. Mysterious grunting noises and the sound of stone grating on stone filtered up from the deep below. The boy was intrigued; as soon as he had the chance, he went back to spy on the mysterious hole and saw two men lowering a bucketful of food down on a rope.

The boy remained out of sight, and when the men were gone, he sneaked up closer. The grunting and scraping noises continued. More curious than scared, he lowered himself down the hole, using the bucket that the men had left behind. Slowly, as his eyes grew accustomed to the dark, the boy was startled by a pair of very blue eyes staring at him intently. They belonged to a muscular man in a loincloth, sporting long white hair and a big bushy beard. The only other object at the bottom of the hole was a huge, seemingly immovable stone.

The blue-eyed man, who was the brother of the reigning monarch, was in fact the rightful king who had reigned previously. His evil brother had deposed him and secretly kept him prisoner for many years. What had kept the rightful king alive, strong, and sane was the one great impediment to his meager comfort: The huge stone he shared his small space with. Every day he wrestled with it, and this made the grating sound the boy had heard. It was through accepting the stone's challenge and making it an ally that this man forged his strength and refined his nobility. Now, through that achievement, he was ready to be resurrected and to regain his throne—a true king at last.

The king was finally brought from the deep place of his

struggle to the surface world, where he was recognized and restored to his throne, while his brother was deposed and thrown behind bars. The point of this story seems to be that there's a nobility deep within each of us that is forged and liberated by our authentic engagement with life's challenges, using them to build new strengths.

The research we mentioned in the last chapter on stress-hardy people who thrive during change showed that they think of ordeals as challenges to learning and growth. People who tend to crumble under stress, on the other hand, view obstacles as threats to the status quo. Reflecting on how you typically view the hurdles in your path is valuable because it gives you insight on whether the stories you tell about your own life center around helplessness or faith.

Faith, in the biblical sense, is the belief in things hoped for but not yet seen. Whether you're hoping to win the World Series, make a difference in the world from a prison cell, or survive a terrible loss like the "King in the Hole" from the tale above, the journey of change always involves overcoming obstacles. When they appear in your path, recognizing them as allies in transformation can help give you the courage you need to respond to life from your highest wisdom.

Reader's Reflection

Think about a difficult situation that you're facing right now. Do you see it as a threat or as a challenge? If it seems to be a threat, imagine ways that it could be a teacher instead. Be specific, and write down your vision for the transformational effects of what seems to be a stone in your path. Then write down the precise behaviors you need to practice in response to it in order to develop your strength.

Chapter 8

Letting Go  and On

GD: Perhaps the beloved Zen teacher Shunryu Suzuki Roshi had it right: We don't need to learn how to let go, we just need to recognize when something is already gone. But that can take time. It entails a gradual process of healing that's different for each one of us before we can move out of the shock of loss and into the transformative period of liminality and return.

On the 11th day of September, 2001, millions of us watched in horror as a man and a woman who were obviously strangers inched toward one another on the impossibly high ledge of a burning skyscraper. Finally, they took one another's hands and leaped together from the flames to their deaths. It seemed that they took our sense of who we were as a nation with them into the abyss aptly named Ground Zero.

Our former sense of American security, pride, and confidence was shaken to the core. We were changed, and have continued to do so ever since. We're still flexing the phantom limb of our once-unquestioned might in a world that has grown too small and interdependent for us to continue acting alone—a world suddenly, and a bit frighteningly, without walls. As a nation, we're still trying to discover who we are and where we are now, often wishing that we could just go back to the way things were. But that can never be.

Whenever life reaches a breaking point like this, what cracks open is always the shell of something larger in us waiting to emerge and take flight. The question wisdom asks of us in situations of such irrevocable loss is: "How can we honor what was, grieve for it, and let go to make room for something new to be born?"

Joan and I facilitated a two-day workshop on change for 35 health professionals and psychologists in December 2004. We began by handing out copies of the tarot's Tower card.

Since 9/11, that timeless archetypal image has taken root in the American psyche. It's usually drawn with a man and a woman falling from the pinnacle of the lightning-struck tower into thin air, into the abyss of separation, loss, and annihilation. Emblematic of sudden change, the image on the card heralds the destruction of an old, familiar form, the irretrievable loss of the way things were perhaps just a fateful moment ago, and the way we were then.

At the workshop, Joan and I asked participants to look at the Tower card and remember a time when their own lives had changed irrevocably in the blink of an eye. Their stories were just like yours or mine: a friend or loved one had died; or a marriage, career position, home, or native land had been painfully relinquished.

Life-changing accidents, illnesses, or national tragedies can turn our world inside out in just a moment's time. Our lives are punctuated with big and little deaths, which are sometimes totally out of the natural order of things, and other times are as natural and necessary as exhaling. Living, after all, is also dying, and finding the grace to do this well takes the mature wisdom of a heart that can tenderly, yet ever so lightly, hold what it most dearly loves.

The Lessons of Grief

The first lesson of loss is the allowance of grief. You might have heard about the animal psychic who was contacted by scientists from a prominent zoo because they were having trouble with the elephants. The giant creatures, taking their cue from the most senior female among them, had stopped obeying commands. Nothing the keepers did got any response, so finally, at their wits' end, they took the unusual step of consulting a psychic.

The woman asked if any elephants might recently have left the zoo and learned that one of them, the oldest female, had been moved away a year or so previously and subsequently died. At the psychic's request, the remains were located and the skull was brought back to the zoo. There, the elephants, especially the senior female who'd had the closest relationship to the dead animal, gathered around and touched the skull with their sensitive trunks while giving full expression to their grief. Once this was accomplished, they returned to their former state of compliance with their keepers, and life at the zoo resumed its normal flow.

Before the elephants could continue with life, they first had to honor the loss of a dear companion. And so it is with

human beings. Allowing time to grieve what was, and to honor its spirit and continuing role in our life, is essential wisdom for making the Hero's Journey home. Trauma specialists like Peter Levine, author of *Waking the Tiger,* know that when it flows, life is a continually self-renewing stream of energy, charging and discharging. But when something so devastating crosses our path that we're overwhelmed by it and can't physiologically discharge in response, the stream turns into a whirlpool that holds us back and wears us down. Stress-related illnesses become common at such times, and zest for beginning creative new initiatives wears thin.

Life is renewed only when held energy can leave our bodies, often in the form of discharged emotion such as the tears of grief or the physical shaking of fear. Letting go is initially just this: a physical exhalation of held energy. Bioenergetic psychologist Alexander Lowen defined freedom as the absence of inner restraint to the flow of feeling. Imagine yourself as having an interior zoo effectively shut down by powerful elephants of restraint, and then imagine the enormous relief when that immovable power is finally set free.

The timing for letting go is a highly individual matter. I think of Native Americans who participate in the Sun Dance, a ritual performed for the freedom of all people. A rawhide cord, attached to the top of the sturdy Sun Dance Pole, is hooked by bear claws through the pectoral muscles of the dancer's chest. The dancer circles 'round and 'round the pole, chanting and praying to the Creator and the ancestors, sometimes pulling away and increasing his pain, sometimes drawing near and prolonging it. At the ultimate moment of readiness—whether it's brought on by prayer, grace, pain, trance, or the support of allies in the circle—the dancer breaks free.

In a similar way, grief is a process of coming close to our pain and then pulling back a little. There's no prescription for how long grieving is supposed to last. We break free when some combination of time, grace, and mindfulness come together to create enough space to hold on to the memory of what's dear without losing ourselves to it. And that's a fine distinction.

When we can't let go, some part of us turns into a pillar of salt, just like Lot's wife. Whatever we can't let go of holds on to us in an eerily ghostly way, so that we, for however long the holding lasts, become ghosts of ourselves. We become what we behold—so if it's the dying past we continue to look upon, we feel perpetually as though a part of *us* is also dying.

I spoke to an Israeli man who'd lost his only son in a suicide bombing and whose life had effectively stopped at that point. He angrily said that he couldn't "move on" with his life, as others had advised, because nothing could "replace" his son—nothing! He was right, since nothing ever could replace his son, but he was also wrong. To move on doesn't mean to replace, or to cherish less, the memory of those who are dear to us. *Moving on isn't disloyalty.* It's not a failure to acknowledge the ways in which our lives have been indelibly touched and enriched by whom or what we loved.

There's a wooden plaque on my office door that reads: "Whatever we love becomes part of us." What we love, and therefore honor, helps make us who we are now. We can't ever let go of that, any more than a tree could let go of the sun, rain, earth, or wind that nourished and grew it.

Learning the Lessons Firsthand

My own experience of grief as an honoring and letting go came through my mother's death. She died when I was two and a half years old, and for nearly my entire life, I'd held an image of myself as unable to move from her grave (my own ground zero, into which all of life's sweetness had vanished). I couldn't leave because I couldn't abandon the one who'd been most dear to me in the entire world—and all that she represented. Yet I couldn't stay because she was no longer there. I was a captive, clinging to her in the surrogate form of her poignantly held absence.

Not until I could finally respond to a spiritual friend's wise counsel to let my mother go was I free to move on in my journey and learn that all the love in the universe hadn't died with her. It was at that moment of letting go that the void of emptiness—which is what I feared most and why I clung for so long—suddenly transformed into a vast spaciousness so utterly suffused with Presence that the illusion of separation, of time and space itself, dissolved into a universe of pure and boundless intimacy.

I can't claim credit for this letting go and the awakening to true nature that it ushered in. After all, for some people grief is a gradual process of letting go, sputtering along in fits and starts. For others, like me, it's a grace that comes like a bolt of lightning. Yet for all of us, grieving requires loving support and the courage to be present to our feelings with great compassion.

There's no shortcut to grieving: It's a journey of its own that's not over 'til it's over. But often we meet an angel or two along the way, a person who, like my friend, will offer a simple insight that falls on fertile ground. A loving comment can drop into the waiting heart like a catalyst and turn base metal suddenly into gold.

· ● ·

Reader's Reflection

What are some of your ways of holding on to the past? What keeps you from letting go? What experience do you have of letting go and moving on that might help you?

Chapter 9

Faith: What's *God* Got to Do with It?

That iconic moment when the two strangers inched toward each other, held hands, and jumped from a ledge on 9/11 was a test of faith for many of us who watched it happen. For some it was a triumph of love and the nobility of the human spirit. Even in death, they testified, our instinct is to reach out toward one another and connect. But for others the death of these two innocents—before our very eyes, no less—seemed like a monstrous outrage that dashed all possibility of faith in a loving God.

When things fall apart, most people discover that questions about faith take center stage. Even without tragedy, one of the earliest inquiries we make in life is about where we come from, why we're here, and what will happen to us when we die. Putting ourselves right with death is one of the most essential forms of wisdom that encourages a compassionate and meaningful life.

The first stages of faith, which continues to mature as we test our beliefs against experience, are based on hopes in which we can take refuge. These help us make peace with impermanence and suffering, and they tend to be fixed and unquestioned until some kind of tragedy says, "Hey, wait a minute here. This doesn't compute!" Life humbles us, defeats our presumptions, and finally breathes into our faith, making it alive. Albert Einstein believed that the most important question we can ask is: "Is the universe friendly?" Living in a world where terror, hatred, and cruelty co-exist with love and beauty is the ultimate paradox that our faith can gradually grow big enough to hold.

Part of the journey of faith may be anger at a God Who we feel has let us down. But Who is that God, anyway? This question itself is holy ground, a place that we can't afford to either trample or leave unexplored. The insights that await us about God, in the depths of our own fully lived experience, become like angels that walk with us on our journey. Those insights are spiritual in nature, rather than a rote part of religious doctrine. They're sacred to us because we live them, not because somebody else told us that they were the right way to believe.

Physician and author Rachel Naomi Remen, M.D., makes an excellent distinction between religion and spirituality. She defines religions as sets of doctrines and dogmas that are designed as bridges to the spiritual—sometimes they get us there, and sometimes they don't. The danger comes in getting attached to the bridge, rather than crossing over it. That's when the dark side of religion shows itself. Although the spiritual ideal is love and forgiveness, religion has been the most reliable source of persecution and genocide since recorded history began.

Many religious people, of course, are deeply spiritual and well nourished by their tradition and have crossed the bridge to compassion, presence, service, and love. But others stay clinging fearfully to a flawed bridge, unable to move across it. One of the many gifts of change is a clear snapshot of where—and on what bridge—we're on.

One religious researcher explored the different ways that people of the same religion think about God. (He chose to study 100 Roman Catholics, since they all learn the same Baltimore

Catechism and technically have similar beliefs, but a study of 100 people from any faith tradition would presumably show the same results.) The researcher found that the higher a person's self-esteem was, the more likely he or she was to believe in a loving God. When self-esteem was low, the tendency was to imagine God in the likeness of a punitive parent.

In Genesis, it's written that human beings are created in the image of God. But the converse is also true—we create our personal images and beliefs about God in our own image, or more specifically, in the image of our parents. One study of fire-and-brimstone preachers, for example, found that a significant number had been abused as children. Like all abused children, their wounds are of spirit as well as flesh, and they'll get handed down from generation to generation until healing interrupts the dark inheritance.

When substantial ordeals challenge our beliefs, childhood ideas about God have a chance to heal and evolve.

JB: I took care of an AIDS patient named Mark, a young man whose experience is still deeply affecting me 20 years after his death. I once asked him, "People often have some theory about why they get sick. Have you been thinking about that question?" and he answered by telling me a heart-rending story about the evolution of his faith.

Mark's father was a fundamentalist preacher who believed that gay people were sinners and affronts to God. Since Mark had known that he was gay since adolescence, he was deeply confused about how an omnipotent and loving God could have created him in a way that was wrong and sinful. Unable to resolve the conflict, Mark did what a lot of people do: He put the black-and-white God of childhood behind him. But rather than inquire into the nature of creation as he got older, he just buried the whole painful problem.

Once he was diagnosed with AIDS, Mark regressed back to his childhood beliefs (which is something we all do). Consequently, he'd come to believe that his father was right: Being gay amounted to spitting in God's face, so He had sent AIDS as a punishment to the sinners, like a modern version of Sodom and Gomorrah.

"Doesn't your God have mercy?" I asked.

"Of course, but you have to repent first," whispered Mark, "and I can't repent of loving [my partner]. He's the best thing that ever happened to me, and I'll love him always—even in the eternal fires of hell."

Rather than moving beyond the shell of his childhood faith and inquiring into it, Mark did an abrupt about-face to avoid the pain: He adopted a new faith that could instantly make him feel safe and whole. Suddenly, God had nothing to do with his situation; God didn't even exist. AIDS was simply a symptom of deficient self-love, so if Mark just learned to love himself, he'd surely be cured. His old faith in a punitive God and his new belief in the power of self-love had something very deep in common: Both revolved around the inner feelings of guilt about being gay that he'd carried since childhood.

In Mark's old belief system, God was punishing him; in his new belief system, he was punishing himself. In both cases, if he could just be good enough, then he'd finally be saved—both his heavenly Father and his earthly father would love him.

But when Mark's illness progressed, he was thrown back into his initial confusion. Self-love hadn't cured him, so perhaps God was punishing him after all. He found out that both his old and new ideas about God were just hollow shells, easily cracked. When the emptiness inside was revealed, Mark began to ask at a deeper level what the story of his life meant.

Just as we have a basic instinct to survive—to breathe, eat, drink, mate, and rest—we have a basic will to search for meaning. It's what makes us essentially human. This need is more compelling, and ultimately more satisfying, than the need for power or achievement. Psychiatrist Viktor Frankl, who survived internment in four Nazi concentration camps, found that the meaning people gave to their suffering either ignited the will to live or contributed to helplessness and death.

When things fall apart, there's an intense need to decode the hidden mystery of love and the paradox of pain. But since we can't know the shape of mystery, the meaning we make may be more about asking questions than finding answers.

In *Letters to a Young Poet,* Rainer Maria Rilke wrote the following:

> I would like to beg of you, dear friend, as well as I can, to have patience with everything that remains unsolved in your heart. Try to love the *questions themselves,* like locked rooms and like books written in a foreign language. Do not now look for the answers. They cannot now be given to you because you could not live them. It is a question of experiencing everything. At present you need to *live* the question. Perhaps you will gradually, without even noticing it, find yourself experiencing the answer, some distant day.

Being friends with the unknown, with the sure knowledge that we don't know how things will turn out, means learning to take refuge in the moment-by-moment unfolding of what is, rather than a belief in what may or may not come to be. Faith based on inquiry, on the willingness to live the questions, requires us to be warriors of the heart. Rather than trusting in God to make everything all right, faith is a trusting that things are, at some level, *already* all right. This permission to let life unfold without judging it is what gives our love a chance to fully flower.

No matter what happens, our most essential human dignity—the capacity to create meaning—can never be taken away. It's always possible to find meaning that connects us to a hidden flow of grace and purpose in the universe, and bears testimony to our full humanity. But that meaning can't just be made up or adopted from an outside source, any more than a caterpillar can paste on butterfly wings and fly. It has to develop organically from deep inquiry into our experience. Allowing that development is the essence of faith.

Faith is not a noun, a thing that we can know for certain, an outcome sure to please. Faith is a verb, our willingness to experience life as it unfolds in all of its pain and all of its promise.

Reader's Reflection

Use Albert Einstein's famous question for inquiry: Do *you* think that the universe is friendly? How do you define faith, and how does that affect the way that you move through the different stages of the three-part rite of passage?

_____

_____

_____

_____

_____

_____

_____

Chapter 10

Holding
Things  *Lightly*

GD: In the movie *Harold and Maude,* Maude's exuberant response to the dumb-founded look on young Harold's face after she's just tossed his engagement ring into the ocean is that she did it so she'd "always know where it is."

Here, the eternally youthful Maude, a wise woman in her 70s, shows the serious young Harold the secret of her joy. Her ability to live life to the fullest comes down to the fact that she knows how to hold whatever life brings to her lightly—with an open heart free of attachment.

She can do this because she's always known who she is: a natural, purely and simply herself. This simplicity of being means that Maude is comfortable in her own skin, with no need for possessions to mirror her self-worth.

But just because Maude holds everything lightly (including herself) doesn't mean that she's uncaring. Quite the opposite—it's only because she doesn't grasp and squeeze the life out of things that she's able to delight so fully in the evanescent forms of life's passing flow. To feel everything deeply, yet not to suffer because of clinging, is the wisdom of non-attachment.

When Joan and I were first falling in love, we had frequent moments that were so very meaningful . . . and we still do. Meeting late in life has a peculiar grace because you're so aware that time is limited and that death will lay claim to one of you sooner rather than later. Each meeting of our eyes was, and still remains, both precious and poignant for this very reason. It feels as though she and I are shimmering and delicately held like the momentary shapes of water in two separate raindrops, falling together—knowing that we're falling—and that these shapes, these forms we recognize as one another, can't last. Staying present to this precious ache remains our constant practice.

The pain and the ecstasy of an open heart are inseparable. "Death," wrote the poet Wallace Stevens, "is the mother of beauty." How much could the ripe pear on the bending branch affect us if it could never fall, if it simply hung there forever, destined to gather dust? To cling, to grasp, to hold on, and to fixate is to dull the organs of our appreciation and caring. Whatever we attempt to take out from the passing stream of life we end up taking for granted. The tightly closed hand becomes the emblem of a tightly closed life. A veil of familiarity drops like a mistaken final curtain over a world that's continuing to unfold in endless wonder.

What the Nun Taught Me

Holding things lightly isn't a skill or technique—it's simply the humble recognition that "these things don't belong to me." Only in this state of holy poverty can life offer us its riches. The open hand that lets go with ease receives just as easily.

I remember a gray, dingy day when I'd gone to the hospital to visit my dying father. I'd brought him a bouquet of colorful flowers, but was shocked to find his room empty. Had he died so soon and been taken away? When I found that he'd been returned to his nursing home, I wandered back down into the busy intersection outside, disoriented and still clutching the bouquet. What could I do with it? An aluminum trash barrel beckoned obscenely . . . but no, I couldn't. These flowers represented my love for my father.

I tried to give them away, first to a woman walking toward me, then to another just getting out of her car. Both of them looked at me as though I were a menacing madman, and both fled fearfully after refusing my gift.

I looked across to the far corner of the intersection and spotted a tiny, hunched nun. As the traffic lights changed, she hobbled across the street, turned, and slowly inched toward where I stood near the curb. Beneath her habit, her face was as brown and withered as a Navajo mummy unearthed from a dry desert cave. When she reached me, I held out the bouquet and asked, "Sister, would you like these flowers?" Without breaking stride, she reached up, gracefully taking the bouquet from me. Her ancient face lit up, and her eyes and smile broadcasted pure radiance. "Thank you," she said, and walked on.

I was blessed and stunned in the same instant. How had she been able to receive in a way the other two women couldn't? And then I realized that this was what her life's learning was all about: trusting, receiving, and appreciating the grace that offered itself freely, here and now, as she lived her unencumbered life.

I know that my uncloistered life could be very similar—yet I also understand that holding things lightly is no sure way to preempt the possibility of grief. We naturally want to preserve and hold on to what touches us most deeply, even if it's just a glimmering moment we'd like to see last. I think of my son Ben's little hands holding onto my forehead as I carried him on my shoulders as a toddler, or of my noble dog Bear—my best friend ever—following me on that last painful run around the lake before I took him to be put down at the vet's. And I think of the ways my father showed his love for me.

Often it's only the most poignant realization of impermanence that opens the heart to love. This brings with it an accompanying sense of loss. It could only be otherwise if we were shallow and uncaring, untouched by life and cut off from our feelings. The grace that brings the unique light of each new moment and the loss we experience with its fading away are but two sides of a single reality, the ebb and flow of life's ocean. Tenderness—which, far more than reason, is what makes us human—refers both to the fullness *and* the woundedness of an open heart. It's loving what must inevitably be let go of.

And this, with all the courage it takes, is how we must hold those dearest to us. Author and spiritual teacher Stephen Levine has worked extensively with grieving parents who have suffered the tragic death of a child. In one of his talks to them, Stephen held up a delicate crystal wineglass with lovely etching. This glass, he told the parents, was precious and fragile, just as their dear lost children had once been and as those surviving still were. It wasn't a question as to *whether* this glass would some-day be broken, but simply *when*. Given its fragility, its eventual destruction was assured. Nevertheless, knowing this, knowing the end was coming, he could still drink from it. Filling the glass from a pitcher of fresh water, he proceeded to do so, with a truly spiritual sense of appreciation. This, he said, is how we should hold and drink from the preciousness our children bring to our lives for however long they may be with us.

Holding lightly and drinking in this way is an act of com-munion that transforms time, bringing us into kairos, the eternal now of pure presence, even if only for a moment. Still, in that moment, we know life's heart . . . and we need not ever forget.

Reader's Reflection

Think of what is most precious to you today. How are you holding it? What experience do you have, or can you imagine, of your heart's being free of attachment?

_____

_____

_____

_____

_____

_____

_____

_____

Chapter 11

How Stressed *Out* Am I?

JB: Traveling through the liminal stage of the Hero's Journey is a lot like going on what Native Americans call a *vision quest*. It involves facing both inner and outer ordeals and, if all goes well, emerging with new strengths. Just surviving the transition between past and future, and coping with the loss and confusion that change brings on, takes a lot of energy. Undergoing transformation requires even more. Cultivating the warrior's courage to stay present to your unfolding flow of experience is an exacting, and sometimes exhausting, task.

And if you let yourself get stressed out and depleted on the journey, vision is much harder to find and claim.

Part of the practical wisdom of dealing with change is to stay aware of just how stressed you are so that you can avoid going off the deep end. That's a practice that involves mindfulness as well as discipline. What are your moods like, for instance? If you're feeling irritable and are blowing things out of proportion, sometimes the most basic tension-reducing tools, such as getting more exercise and sleep, can restore you to balance. This may seem like mundane wisdom, but transformation is out of the question if you're throwing a tantrum.

When I was the director of a stress-disorders clinic at a Harvard Medical School teaching hospital during the 1980s, we kept a close eye on how much stress patients were experiencing. It turns out that if you add up how many changes people have to cope with, you'll get a pretty good idea of how much psychological and physiological strain their system is under. The actual strain varies with a person's coping skills of course, but change scales are still a good starting point.

Medical researchers Thomas Holmes and Richard Rahe devised the first scale of common life changes in the 1960s, called the Life Changes Stress Test, with the hope of quantifying how stress impacts health. They found that the more change a person has to cope with, the more likely they are to get sick. Most everyone has experienced this. Stress initiates a fight-or-flight response in the body, which prepares every system to meet unusual challenges, whether they're physical realities or psychological fears. The result of too much fight-or-flight can be elevated blood pressure, irregular heartbeats, muscle tension, breathing problems, digestive disturbances, head-aches, and immune dysfunctions that make you more prone to allergies, autoimmune illnesses, or infection.

Holmes and Rahe gave each event the measurement of a life change unit (LCU). For example, death of a spouse, which is considered the most disruptive of all life changes, rates 100 LCUs; while minor violations of the law, such as getting a parking ticket, rate 5 LCUs. But even positive changes like getting married (50 LCUs) or having an outstanding personal achievement (25 LCUs) can upset the status quo and create stress while you adjust to the new circumstance. Writing a book, in my estimation, ranks at about 75 LCUs. Writing a book with the spouse you've just married, as in the case with Gordon and me, is just plain over the top.

People who score high on life change (250 LCUs or above)

are generally more prone to physical illness and psychological distress than people with lower scores. But even life-change scores can't possibly tell the whole story. The meaning of the changes we experience can either decrease their disruptiveness or increase it.

For instance, I remember a patient who checked off "change in religious beliefs" when given the Holmes-Rahe Life Changes Stress Test to fill out. When he and I discussed it, the patient spoke about being a recent immigrant from Haiti, where he'd been raised in the vodun (voodoo) religion. After coming to the United States, he met and married a woman who was a Jehovah's Witness, so he converted. Well, the two religions couldn't be more diametrically opposed, and the man was experiencing tremendous inner turmoil as he wrestled with his beliefs. In his case, the point score assigned to the life change seriously underestimated the readjustment that a recent change in religious beliefs required.

When the scale was created in the 1960s, there were no categories for modern events such as terrorist attacks, blended families, teenage children with multiple body piercings, major computer crashes, and corporate downsizing. Holmes and Rahe, in fact, estimate that life is 44 percent more difficult now than it was 50 years ago. And it seems to be getting more challenging by the minute as we form a global community. In addition to keeping up with the political and social implications of events happening in dozens of foreign countries, just keeping up with e-mail can be stressful. Technology is changing so fast that soon only human beings under the age of ten will have the advanced neural circuitry required to use the remote control on the VCR.

You may want to Google the Holmes-Rahe scale and find out just how tense you really are. But don't worry if you don't have time. Research shows that one of the best measures of stress is to draw a line on a piece of paper and mark the left end "1" and the right end "10." Then decide where on the line your stress level falls, between the Great Calm of 1 and the Great Upset of 10, and make a mark. That's called a *visual analog scale*.

Right now, having had less than six hours of sleep last night, I rate about a 7. And in my experience, that's too high a stress level to either feel happy or to do any kind of decent work, so I'm going to have to forsake the computer for a brisk walk in the mountain air, in the hopes that I'll return with a stress level below 5.

Now while these particular numeric levels make sense to me, only *you* can figure out what each number corresponds to in your own experience. If you get into the habit of using this simple scale, you'll soon get a feel for your normal stress levels, for those that correspond to optimal performance and flow, and for those that tell you you're over your personal stress limit. The challenge is to reduce your stress in general, and in particular during times of change, so that you'll be available for the wisdom and transformation that can accompany these disruptive times.

My books *Inner Peace for Busy People* and *Inner Peace for Busy Women* are filled with simple strategies to center yourself. Managing stress doesn't have to be an elaborate undertaking—it's primarily a matter of common sense. Aerobic exercise is probably the fastest way to counter it, but even a 30-minute walk, a 20-minute period of yoga or meditation, or half an hour of listening to classical music can reduce tension levels substantially.

In the development of body wisdom, just as for mental wisdom, the key to progress is *self-reflection*. You can't reduce the stress of change to a level where your highest self becomes accessible unless you notice when it's risen too high. The wisdom, then, is simple: Take a break. Get some rest. Do something nourishing that reminds you that life is worth living and that beneath the veneer of stress, a world of wonder awaits your return.

· • ● • ·

Reader's Reflection

On a scale of 1 to 10, where 1 is calm and 10 is ultimately tense, how stressed do you feel right now? What's one simple thing you can do for yourself when your stress level gets too high and compromises your ability to cope? What keeps you from doing it when you know that you need a break?

_____

_____

_____

_____

_____

_____

_____

_____

Chapter 12

The *Wisdom* of Not Doing

JB: Facing the unknown is so frightening for most of us that we'll do just about anything to find our bearings and feel secure again. There can be survival wisdom in that: Going through the motions of daily life after a traumatic loss, for example, provides a stable framework to hold on to when it feels like you're walking through the maelstrom.

But keeping busy can also become a prison, an attachment to an old way of thinking and acting that blocks access to new vision. When that happens and you find yourself walking in circles around your fears, the wisdom of transition is to do what's totally counterintuitive: nothing. Just rest and wait until you find your bearings.

Here's an example of what I mean from my journal.

I'm sitting at the kitchen table with Gordon, trying to force myself to figure out how to proceed next with this book. I want to know what the score is, to be in charge, to feel safe and efficient, worthy of the trust that the publisher has placed in us to write this book together. But we've reached a monumental impasse: We've just finished reading the first draft and had a come-to-Jesus meeting. It's too preachy and how-to, a glorified advice column. For my part, I've fallen back on the gods of research and glib counsel, giving the impression that there's some magic formula that can instantly transform the fear and confusion that are part of the natural habitat where change works its dark magic.

The urge to do-do-do, to fix the book right now, to get out of the darkness of uncertainty into the light of wisdom and accomplishment, grabs me by the limbic system. I'm fearful of missing the deadline, of discovering that the muse has deserted me, of botching up our marriage in this, our first big project together. A very old and primitive part of my nervous system—the reptilian brain—takes over. I go into survival mode and begin defending myself. At that moment I'm quite sure that this impasse is all Gordon's fault. He's hoping for authentic wisdom and fine writing. I'm hoping for a simple book that's practical and comforting. So far, neither of us has reached our objective, and I regress to tears and blame. This is not my best self, but I'm a woman possessed by fear who has lost her center.

I want to run back to the computer and begin writing right away, even though Gordon has made the point that we need to back up and get some distance first. Otherwise, all our efforts will amount to rearranging the deck furniture on the *Titanic,* rather than putting the ship on the right course. I'm feeling desperate and want to calm myself by doing something, even when I know that the result will likely be more of the same.

Gordon does for me what I can't seem to do myself, even though I know what's needed. He asks what would feel nurturing: A walk? A hot bath? A good book? Like an angry child I leap on each suggestion and jump up and down on it until it's pulverized. He stays calm and present throughout my tirade, holding for me what I can't hold for myself. Fortunately, he doesn't mistake this hissing shrew of a woman for who I really am. Held in the safe harbor of his calm, my emotions begin to subside, and I remember that the essential wisdom of transition isn't just a piece of advice for a how-to book. It can be embodied, known, and moved into right now.

Stanza 15 of Stephen Mitchell's translation of the classic wisdom text *Tao Te Ching* poses a delicious and instructive question:

"Do you have the patience to wait
till your mud settles and the water is clear?
Can you remain unmoving
till the right action arises by itself?"

We can all wait gracefully sometimes, letting the water clear. But stress is a saboteur that keeps stirring things up again. The more tense I feel, the less capable I am of letting go and allowing the water to settle. I get into the Chinese-finger-trap mentality.

You see, when I was little, my father used to bring home those colorful woven cylinders of straw. I'd stick a finger in each end, and then when I tried to pull them out, I'd be stuck. The harder I pulled, the tighter the trap closed around me. Good dad that he was, my father used these simple toys to teach me that whenever I was feeling stuck, the best thing to do was just let go. And as soon as my fingers relaxed and I stopped struggling, I was free.

When I was a stress researcher, we used fancy words for letting go and coming back to center—for freedom from the finger trap of the mind—such as *self-regulation*. That's a nice, descriptive term because it implies that you've been regulated by something outside yourself, or at least by something outside your true nature, even if it's your own old stories and childhood conditioning. Self-regulation leads to self-possession.

Sometimes this skill is called knowing how to comfort or nurture yourself, but the paradox in self-nurturing is that while it feels great, there's a lot of resistance to doing it when you're scared. It seems counterintuitive. *If a lion were chasing me, I'd run*, you might think, *not drop to the ground and serenely meditate*. While that's an extreme and unrealistic example, I think you know what I mean. An ongoing inquiry for me concerns how to transcend this paradox: How can I be authentically present to my feelings—for instance, fear—and also relax and comfort myself simultaneously? That's the only way to honor my experience. To do less is to pretend that things are different from how they are. And rejecting the truth only leads to muddier water.

So, getting back to where we started with the Great Book Meltdown, I took my miserable self downstairs to the bath that Gordon had so kindly drawn for me. Classical music and a little incense created a comforting environment, and as I sat in the tub, I let myself be aware of what I was experiencing without trying to change or judge it. But instead of focusing on my thoughts about the situation, which were reruns of the same story I'd been trapped in for hours, I shifted attention to my body: What were the actual sensations in my cells and tissues? What did the energy feel like? Where was it flowing, and where was it stuck? In this way I could stay mindful of my authentic experience but simultaneously transcend the linear way that the story had held my attention with the efficiency of a finger trap.

When we're in the transitional time between "no longer" and "not yet," it's natural for fears to surface—after all, they're sustained by the ego's familiar stories of separation and unworthiness. When the Israelites gained freedom from the Pharaoh and escaped from servitude in Egypt, they had to wander in the desert for 40 years until they finally entered the Promised Land. Forty years is two generations—it took that long for the old stories of slavery, and perhaps even the desire to return to what was terrible but familiar, to lose their grip. Then the muddy water could finally clear.

When that happens, it's much easier to see the way, to get our bearings, and to have patience with all that's unknown . . . which, in the final analysis, is everything outside our immediate experience.

· ●●● ·

Reader's Reflection

What obstacles get in the way of your taking a rest and letting go?
What could you do, or not do, right now that would bring you peace?

_____

_____

_____

_____

_____

_____

_____

_____

Chapter 13

Vanquishing the *False* Self

JB: People bond when life gets rough because they get real. In a room full of people who are grieving, there's fear, anger, sorrow . . . and tenderness. There's just no energy left to wear a mask, so people come as they are. They're their unadorned, vulnerable selves. The false self, which exists as a response to the deep fear that we're unlovable, gets knocked off its pedestal when things fall apart. But when the immediate crisis passes, the tendency is for the ego to reconfigure itself and for the masks to go back on.

In order for the real self that emerges during change to become established as a steady state, it's important to understand how the false self works. Then we can see through the fears that maintain it and find the courage and skillfulness to remain the person who we really are.

Buddhist teacher Pema Chödrön defines the essence of fearlessness (or bravery) as being without self-deception. The willingness to look at ourselves and face what's inside takes courage because we're bound to discover things that we don't like. There's no hiding or denial for the brave. The catch-22 is that we don't know what it is that we're unwilling to see. The ego is clever, and whatever makes it cringe in shame gets shoved under the covers. The only way that we can reclaim whatever it's holding hostage under there is to be aware of our judgments about other people. They hold the key to what we judge most harshly about ourselves.

Again, here's an example from my journal to further illustrate what I mean:

> I'm talking to a friend about the service project of a mutual acquaintance, who always goes out of his way to do good things for people. What comes out of my mouth is a little bit crude and shocking—there's force behind it. I say

something snippy and judgmental like, "Give me a break. I don't think his true concern is for the people he's helping at all. I really think he's just a spiritual grandstander, more interested in the glorified do-gooder image these projects reflect on him than anything else."

Immediately I feel ashamed and realize that I've just made a mean-spirited projection. I'm not privy to this man's motivation at all, but I do know that *I* sometimes do things to look good to other people because it makes me feel better about myself. Since we've been taught that mixed motives are suspect (after all, we should all be evolved to the point of selfless sainthood), admitting to them is hard if you've got a strong superego—an inveterate inner critic who keeps your unruly instincts strictly in line.

All human beings tuck the behaviors, desires, and emotions that make them feel ashamed into their shadow, which is invisible because it's out of our visual field. Poet Robert Bly compares it to a long bag we drag behind us: If we could look inside, we'd see that it contains all the disowned parts of ourselves that anybody we ever wanted to please—parents, clergy, teachers, lovers—may have criticized. In order to get their love, we became separate from ourselves.

The process of sealing off shame involves deep denial—an

out-of-sight, out-of-mind strategy that enables us to feel super-ficially okay. But were the false self ever to meet up with the contents of that bag, the result would be paralyzing humilia-tion of the most overwhelmingly devastating order. Whatever is being denied builds up a head of steam in the unconscious; and often releases itself in embarrassing, revealing, and self-sabotaging ways.

The late family therapist Virginia Satir compared the contents of the human shadow to a pack of dogs scratching at the cellar door, trying to get out. It takes a lot of energy to keep leaning on the door, but the dogs will escape anyway, in spite of your best efforts to keep them in the basement. And their most common escape route is through projections.

So if you're a sweet person who doesn't feel safe expressing your anger, you may think that you don't even have that emo-tion. Instead, you'll project it onto other people who seem mad to (or at) you. Everywhere your mild eyes rest, scary rage will stare back at you. And if you're incapable of intimacy, perhaps you'll accuse your partner of being unable to relate to you. Projecting is the way that the ego, the judgmental false self, maintains its separateness and cuts itself off from kairos and the greater flow of consciousness that's the essence of all that is.

When I accused a man I hardly knew of being a self-interested, spiritual do-gooder, it was my frightened, shame-filled shadow that was doing all the talking. When I admitted the projection to a friend, she put the incident into a wise and loving perspective: "Hey, you're only human, Joanie," she reassured me. "I feel very close to you when you share your feelings with me the way that you just did. I know I can trust you because you're willing to look at yourself and tell the truth, rather than pretending to be perfect. Your being real is much more important to me than your trying to be Mother Teresa."

Moving Away from Judgment

Being without self-deception requires the deliberate willingness to own our projections and to be a whole, real person, neuroses and all. This is a useful practice to undertake. You'll notice that when you're relaxed and centered, there's much less of a tendency to project. Therefore, the best time to identify projections is when you're tired and stressed—when the mean streak is most likely to come out.

For example, sometimes when my plane lands in the Denver airport after a long trip, I'm surprised at my own unkindness. My mind runs a snide commentary on other people's assorted shortcomings: All of a sudden I'm the clothes police, the diet squad, and the relationship gestapo. When that happens, my first reaction is to judge myself and create even more shame and separation.

Instead of self-judgment, courage requires that we meet our projections with gentleness and compassion. You're feeling mean? Okay, so be it, as long as you don't act out or hurt someone else's feelings. By the end of a projection-fest at the airport, I've become so painfully aware of how important a good image is to me, and how vulnerable I am to criticism, that it breaks my heart. Stopping to sense myself, I can feel the echoes of a lonely childhood whispering a soft lament deep within my cells. A lump forms in my throat and tears well up behind my eyes. The compassion that I feel for myself at that moment turns into a presence that spills over, and I'm possessed by an overwhelming love for the people I was just criticizing. After all, we're so very much alike. We're just human beings doing our best to be loved.

When I was a young person, the concept of self-realization

seemed abstract and unattainable. I'd gotten the odd idea that it was some kind of grandiose spiritual super-orgasm where the music of the spheres played, and one entered a state of perpetual bliss. Now there are certainly states of consciousness where that kind of experience happens, but self-realization is a much more down-to-earth process. It just means that you're willing to inhabit your whole self, with all its peculiar shades of gray.

Remembering to Be Ourselves

There's a wonderful Hasidic teaching tale about Rabbi Zusya, who tries all his life to be a good and righteous man. When he finally dies (no doubt exhausted from all his trying) and stands before God, the Creator says, "Zusya, it's clear that you were an absolutely fabulous human being, as wise as Solomon and as brave as David. But tell me, why is it that you weren't ever able to be Zusya?"

In other words, if we're just ourselves, we're afraid that won't be enough. But here's the rub: People who are real and flawed often seem more lovable than those who give off an air of perfection. I'm reminded of the study in which research psychologists showed students one of two pictures. They were of the same well-dressed woman, but in one photo she'd just spilled a cup of coffee in her lap. The students reported liking the woman with a lapful of coffee much better than her clean counterpart.

The sad truth is that the false self isn't inherently likable, no matter how hard it tries. It's just too rigid and self-righteous. It's easier to like people who are natural—that is, transparent and unaffected. I'm sure that scientists will someday discover the part of the brain where the "bullshit detector" resides because we've all got one. People who project an idealized image make us uncomfortable—they're just too good to be true. And it's hard to make contact with them because their mask is in the way.

However, when people tell us the truth and allow themselves to be vulnerable, then there's someone real to relate to. So being yourself, your own unique Zusya, is an intimate and graceful practice of presence that's simple and easy yet has the power to transform both you and the people around you.

When I facilitate groups, there's often a turning point when someone says something authentic that breaks the ice. Maybe we're talking about meditation, and people are asking polite questions. I move automatically into my teacher mode, and the group then acts like students. We know these roles well—they're practiced and polished—but we're not really connecting with one another. They might as well be reading a book.

Then someone says something like, "My son was diagnosed with schizophrenia a year ago, and I don't think that I'll ever recover from the grief. Can anyone please tell me what surrender means in a situation like this? I'm so damn scared. What good is meditation anyway?"

You can hear a pin drop in the room, and then the held breaths are followed by a collective exhalation. Most people's center of attention drops from their head to their heart, and we all meet there, in that field beyond judgment that the poet Rumi wrote about. At that point a gentleness fills the air, and you can feel the sweetness of compassion running through the room like a warm current. Masks drop, and the conversation grows deep and true.

The courage to be fearless, to be without self-deception, is a simple practice. It doesn't mean being abrasive or without discernment—it just means being vulnerable to yourself, willing to witness what shames you with curiosity and compassion, and being vulnerable to other people when the situation is safe and appropriate.

Reader's Reflection

What's the most common thing you tend to criticize in other people? Form an inquiry about it as if it were a projection. If you tend to see anger, ask, "Why am I so mad?" If you tend to see envy, ask, "Why am I so jealous?" Stick with the question, especially in the moment when you catch yourself in a projection.

Chapter 14

The Synergy of Change: Discovering an  "We"

GD: There was only one time in our relationship—which I'll tell you about in a minute—when Joan wanted to punch me in the nose. The incident revealed something valuable to us both about the nature of relationships, which are perhaps the most conflict-laden, risky, and exacting of all change processes.

The difficulty in this complex dance is how to stay open to, and fluidly engaged with, the other person without losing your own integrity in the bargain. This applies to anyone whom you have an important connection with. If you and that other person can each maintain your own integrity and yet stay open to one another, especially at key decision points, then a new and creative possibility emerges. By including and transcending your differences, you can arrive at something greater than the sum of your individual desires, talents, and efforts.

This new possibility within relationships is a magical transformation known as *synergy,* or the emergence of an authentic and collectively wise "we." It's the equivalent of the grace an orchestra achieves by harmonizing—not neutralizing into sameness—the rich differences of which it's composed. If you and your partner (spouse, colleague, family member, or what have you) aren't successful in this regard, then there's a high probability that either or both of you will take a dangerous step backward. Being overly accommodating and self-sacrificing in order to preserve your relationship at all costs leads to mindless conformity—a false "we" that's not only unconscious but empty. You're not really in there, so all parties stand to lose.

The razor's edge, which marks the dividing line between living an authentic or a false "we," is the degree to which we're willing to risk telling the truth. There can't be an authentic "we" unless each of us is willing to be an authentic "I," truly and transparently ourselves in the other's presence. Of course we don't want to hurt one another, and we don't want to be rejected, abandoned, or punished—these are the risks, the flaming hoops we have to leap through. Our integrity, our unedited wholeness, our truth, and our compassion are what's required of us as individuals if we're to reach the higher level of wholeness that is collective intelligence. If we're not willing to be real, a fiasco is sure to follow, as Joan and I discovered to our great chagrin.

The "Huatulco Moment"

We were vacationing in Huatulco, a small, sleepy town on the Pacific coast of Mexico. It was a Sunday evening, just after dark, and we'd taken a cab to a romantic, ocean-side restaurant we'd heard raves about. Since we were both hungry and the cuisine was supposed to be excellent, we were really looking forward to dining there. Alas, when we arrived and descended the steep steps down to the beach, where the tables and a bar were located, we discovered that the place was closed. Walking back up the staircase and down the other side to the dark, deserted esplanade where the cab had left us earlier, we spied the lights of a restaurant that, our hosts had warned, was notorious for its bad food and exorbitant prices. Yet there were no cabs or even cars passing by, so going somewhere else would take time.

Joan was famished, and her blood sugar was dropping like the stock market after a bubble of irrational exuberance has burst. She wanted to eat immediately, or sooner if possible. In the direction we were already walking, the neon sign of what might be an alternative dining possibility around the bend was glowing and beckoning . . . to *me*, that is. I was the one who cared much more about *what* I ate than when, and despised consuming—and paying for—what would most likely be bad food. I wanted Joan to just make that small extra effort to look around that bend in the road, for her own good (I rationalized) as well as my own. She, however, was loath to continue what she insisted would be a fruitless and exhausting probe into a night of infinite nothingness.

We reached the raised pavement where the restaurant tables, almost all of which were empty, were set like a trap. A white-jacketed waiter—I probably hallucinated his eight legs—hovered at his stand in the center of this clean, well-lighted place, where an iced table displayed impressively large but pathetically limp shrimp. These stale specimens were the evening special . . . at four times the price we'd paid for any other meal in Mexico. Joan ate her flaccid seafood with a combination of relief and—truth be known—resignation. I barely touched mine, as my palate and wallet were both recoiling, seized by the same fit of nausea. Once we'd finished and walked around the aforementioned bend, we saw what the neon sign had been advertising: a pizza parlor. As the delicious mouth-watering fragrance reached us, we saw that the place was just closing. If only . . . damn!

Each of us was quietly seething, intensely disliking the other. I was angry with myself for having accommodated my wife while abandoning my own judgment (after all, nothing rankles like self-betrayal), while she was angry at me for being insensitive to her needs. This may sound like no big deal, but it was the worst meltdown we'd experienced in our young relationship, and it still holds the record by a long shot.

The next morning, we found ourselves the lone breakfast diners on a lovely veranda overlooking a quiet golf course. The coffee was excellent, but the strain was still palpable between Joan and me. I asked if she knew the story of Orpheus; when she said she didn't, I proceeded to render it as dramatically, albeit satirically, as I could.

Orpheus, whose songs were so affecting that they tamed savage beasts, had journeyed down to the underworld to see if he could win back his kidnapped love, Eurydice. The god of the underworld relinquished her on one condition: On the way back up, no matter how piteous her pleas, Orpheus must not turn back to look at Eurydice until both were safely above ground, or he'd lose her for eternity. Eurydice didn't know that by ignoring her urgent requests to turn around and look at her, Orpheus was actually doing what was best for both of them. When he gave in (against his better judgment) and did turn around, the last thing he saw was her horrified face fading back into the underworld, this time forever.

"Hearing that story now, in light of what happened last night," I asked Joan with a mirthful tone of provocation, "how does it make you feel?"

She paused, and then said quite simply, "Like punching you in the face!"

The result was instantaneous: I fell back in my chair, laughing uproariously, and soon Joan was chuckling as well. The patent absurdity of my self-serving "men know best" parable was obvious, and her response had been just what it called for. The tension dissolved.

Our "Huatulco Moment," as we've come to call it, was a minor happening, but it was a great opportunity to learn about interdependence. So we considered this question together: What would have redeemed the previous night's experience, and what might prevent it from happening again? I saw that I could have let Joan know that I fully heard and understood her truth at the time: She was exhausted and uncomfortable, needing immediate relief. But I could also have held to my own truth, perhaps having her take a seat for a moment at the House of Limp Shrimp while letting her know that I wanted to take a look around the bend before settling down. (Also, we decided that we'd carry energy bars so that we wouldn't be pressured into poor dining decisions again.)

Plunging into the Unknown

Every ongoing relationship is a plunge into the unknown, the crucible of change that can potentially bring us into a deeper relationship with ourselves, as well as with each other. In terms of the three-part rite of passage, starting a relationship of any kind marks the departure from what your life was like as a lone individual. Then you go on a pilgrimage to a strange land together, facing ordeals and finding strengths in the transitional time between being an independent "I" and discovering the nature of an interdependent "we." The phase of return, if you make it that far, is a mysterious synthesis in which the two of you maintain your own autonomy yet find yourselves mutually expanded into a larger way of being—what the Germans call *mitsein,* or "being with."

What makes *mitsein* possible is, above all, loving the truth together. When this mutual concern for truth is absent, all you're left with is either impasse or an accommodation that will inevitably feel like self-betrayal and lead to resentment. Nobel Peace Laureate Shirin Ebadi, relating a Persian parable, told an interfaith audience that the truth was once a mirror in the hands of God. The mirror "fell out of God's hands and shattered into millions of pieces. Everyone got a piece, so everyone can claim he has a piece of the truth." Our challenge is to hold up our own piece with courage and fidelity while honoring the pieces held up by others and thus acknowledging the possibility of more completeness.

The word *relationship* comes from the Latin root *relatio,* which means "to tell." So when you *tell* me honestly what's going on inside of you, and I *tell* you what's happening inside me, we're *relating* to one another. Otherwise we're like two closed books sitting side by side. Joan and I, in our "after-action review" on the sunlit veranda, were finally relating to each other, learning from our shared experience . . . and our differences. We were having a truly fine morning meal, even though it involved dining reflectively on the roadkill from our previous night's poor driving.

When both parties are present to each other in this way, willing to be changed in ways that enlarge, not diminish, the completeness of their truth, the relationship gives birth to an authentic "we" with its own vitality and creative identity. As the first-century Jewish sage Rabbi Hillel asked, "If I am not for myself, who will be for me? If I am only for myself, what am I? If not now, when?"

The challenge that relationship creates is to be for yourself in the sense of staying in your own center, while also being there for the other person in a way that respects and supports them. That's a delicate and critical balance between truth and compassion. And, as Hillel implies, there's no time like the present to learn this lesson, perhaps discovering the meaning of love in action in the process.

Reader's Reflection

Think of several situations where you've been in conflict with other people who are important to you. Divide a sheet of paper into two columns: In the left-hand column, describe the situations and what you thought or felt; and in the right-hand column, describe what you actually said or did. Where you see discrepancies, what were the outcomes, and how might it have been different?

_____

_____

_____

_____

_____

_____

_____

_____

Chapter 15

Making a *Difference*

JB: The third part of the rite of passage is the return. Having come through the transition and faced its ordeals, the initiate in the journey of change has a much better understanding of his strengths and gifts. The journey is complete when these are offered to the community, for the good of all. But sometimes the reality that we're just one person can be demoralizing. What can we do, and where should we start?

Here's a pertinent example from my journal, which I wrote in April of 2004.

I'm walking through the airport, and the afternoon news is blaring from a television set overhead. I sit down to wait for my plane and quickly become mesmerized by horrific photos of a smiling young woman in fatigues who's dragging a scrawny, miserable Iraqi man around on a leash. He's naked and humiliated—a human being no matter what the accusations against him might be. But the pixie-faced private can't possibly be seeing him that way: Oblivious to his pain and loss of dignity, she's dehumanized him and also herself. I hide my face in shame for her, and in sadness for the endless suffering that retaliation is doomed to create. Finally, overwhelmed with the horror of it all, I bury my nose in a mystery novel, seeking strange asylum in what will surely amount to more violence.

I'm struck at this moment that I'm not so very different from the smiling young woman holding the leash. I've turned my back on what needs changing because looking at it straight on simply hurts too much. What can I possibly do? Lacking any immediate ideas, I've just numbed out. The compassion of my essential nature has gone missing. And my ego's habitual defenses of denial, blame, and resignation have taken over. I know this . . . I hate this . . . but I keep reading the damn novel anyway.

Later, in the months that follow, I began to reflect on what enlightened social action might be required of me, and what got in the way of developing a vision that might make a difference. It's obvious that numbing out won't help in the vision department, so I began an inquiry process. *What prevents me from taking some kind of action?* I asked myself. And it struck me that the most common, garden-variety adversary of enlightened social action is helplessness: the fear that I really don't have what it takes to make a difference anyway, so why bother?

Helen Keller—who might certainly have spent a lifetime feeling helpless—addressed those feelings directly when she said, "I am only one, but still I am one. I cannot do everything, but I can still do something." Often, when I'm giving seminars around the country, someone will hand me a thank-you note or come over in person to tell me that I've made some substantial difference to their healing. Maybe I can't end the gruesome cycle of killing, dehumanization, and retaliation that has consumed the greater human family since the beginning of recorded history, but I *can* help one family find forgiveness.

As I think of the people whom I've been able to help, I'm reminded of the child who stands at the shoreline tossing beached starfish back into the ocean. When an adult comments that there are too many starfish on the shore to make any difference, the child looks at the starfish in her hand and says, "Well, it makes a difference to this one."

Each one of us has something of value to give. The problem often comes when we think that someone else's gift is more valuable than our own. The great Hindu classic, the Bhagavad Gita, counsels us to do our own duty, since trying to do someone else's places us in great spiritual danger. St. Paul expressed something similar when he spoke of the different gifts of Spirit that each person has. Some of us, for example, have the gift of healing, others are politically savvy; some have the gift of parenting, others of organization. In other words, the question that makes the most sense for me to ask isn't, "Why can't I be more like super-activist Eve Ensler?" it's, "How can I best use the gifts *I've* been given to make a difference in the world?"

When you do what only you can do—instead of trying to do what other people can do—strange and wonderful things often magnify your vision. It's as if the road rises up to meet you and circumstances flow together in a mysterious and elegant way, beyond the scope of your own, individual efforts.

There's a scientific reason why this may be true. In the 1960s, U.S. meteorologist Edward Lorenz was modeling global weather patterns using the largest computers then available for his purpose. He found that the weather system was so permanently in a state of chaos, so inherently unpredictable, that if a monarch butterfly in Mexico were to suddenly flap its wings this way or that, the amplifying turbulence could destabilize weather in faraway places like Outer Mongolia. Chaos theorists have come to call this "The Butterfly Effect." The fact is, when conditions are right and your guidance is clear, only a slight modification in your attitude or intent can change the world around you.

The more the chaos, the greater the possibility that a single individual can make a substantial difference. For example, only when the despotic regime of the Soviet Union was in utter shambles after its rigidly confining order had collapsed could Boris Yeltsin change history with a single act of courage. Facing down the tanks in Red Square, he transformed his nation's future.

Anthropologist Victor Turner called the chaos of liminality, when the old order is gone and the new is still formless, "the realm of the possible." This is the time when whatever we can envision and hope for has the greatest chance of becoming real. If we act on it, this is the moment when unlikely allies and unsuspected resources will arise to strengthen our hand. Chaos holds both of the meanings of *potentia*—"potential" and "power"—and often requires only the slightest effort to actualize enormous shifts.

Reader's Reflection

What gift or strength do you have that could help make the world a better place? Think locally about your own community as you consider this. How could you offer that gift to your community?

_____

_____

_____

_____

_____

_____

_____

Chapter 16

Finding Your *Vision*

GD: There's a fundamental difference between change that "happens to us" and change that we initiate. The distinction lies in our innate human capacity to envision and actualize the potential that lives just beneath the surface of our present reality. Present circumstances, however daunting, always hold this seed of possibility. Perceiving it in a way that focuses and engages our desire to act and make it real for the good of our communities is the very essence of vision, the gift that successfully concludes the threshold stage of a rite of passage.

Offering this gift of vision back to the community is the final act of the three-part rite of passage: the return. The story of an ordinary woman, Bernadette Cozart, is an inspiring example of how any one of us can find and initiate a new vision for the future, even in situations that may appear hopeless.

Bernadette came to Harlem from the Midwest in the early 1980s with a degree in horticulture and her own good heart. The asphalt inner city that greeted her was far from a gardener's paradise: Empty lots filled with garbage, broken glass, and toxic refuse were home to rats, drug dealers, and glassy-eyed addicts. What might have been inviting parks and play areas that were safe for children were instead dangerous pits of hopelessness and despair. Most nearby residents stayed cooped up in their tenement apartments rather than risk passing too close to these perilous haunts.

When Bernadette saw the shape of this heartbreak, she simply could have condemned it and gone about her business; or she could have resigned herself to it, as most of the neighbors had done. But instead, she embodied Mahatma Gandhi's famous affirmation: "We must become the change we want to see."

The combination of Bernadette's past experience, kindness, and active imagination helped her see something beyond the hopelessness and chaos. She had a vision of what the countless rubble-filled lots could be: They could be transformed into community gardens. She also saw that involving neighbors in creating and tending these gardens would bring them out of their tenements, and transform their relationships with one another. With her compelling vision, and the talent and commitment to realize it, Bernadette helped Harlem take a step toward a better future.

At the time that I heard her interviewed on National Public Radio, Bernadette had obtained funding from the adjacently located business community and facilitated the creation of more than 100 community gardens. Elders with farming skills from their rural communities of origin were working side-by-side with neighborhood youth, giving them a life-nurturing alternative to gangs and violence. The gardens were gated, with keys kept by locally appointed stewards. The herbs grown there were packaged and sold, thus bringing some financial return to the community. And wind chimes and garden sculptures, which were gifts of local business owners, beautified the spaces.

When Bernadette showed up in Harlem, its old grandeur had deteriorated into chaos, and rebirth into a new form wasn't yet in sight. This threshold stage, with all its chaos and uncertainty, is a natural testing ground for new vision. The way that ordinary people like Bernadette become social-change agents who "perceive the possible" contains important clues about how the rest of us can develop vision. It's interesting to ask, "What made it possible for her to see hope and life in a situation where other people couldn't?"

In part, Bernadette had moved to Harlem from another place, so she wasn't ground down by a culture of hopelessness. She could see the neighborhood with fresh eyes because she came from "outside the box." That leads to the question, "How can *we* get outside of untenable situations that we've been putting up with day after day as though they were the natural order of things?" The answer has two parts: (1) We have to become conscious of the toll that the situation is taking; and (2) we have to imagine what it would be like to become free from it.

The Brazilian educator Paolo Freire provided a good example of that two-part process. Growing up in one of the country's poorest cities, he observed that people in the barrios seemed incapable of changing their miserable condition because they had no words to even name their predicament. It was all they knew, and as a result of not knowing any differently, they were like the proverbial fish who hasn't yet consciously discovered water. Until they could emerge from what Freire called their "culture of silence," there was no hope for change.

Freire's method of breaking the silence and helping the people become conscious of a situation that was in full sight, yet hidden because it was like water to a fish, consisted of taking photos of different districts. Then he'd invite the people who lived there, along with a team of social scientists, to look at the photos and give them meaning. When they were able to name the terrible conditions for the first time—and their feelings about them—they were no longer unconscious prisoners, identified with the situation. At last, they were able to conceive of, and therefore create, alternatives. The fish had discovered water.

Appreciative Inquiry

Naming is a self-reflective wisdom process that allows us to emerge from bondage. Contemporary French philosopher Paul Ricoeur wrote that "language is the light of the emotions. Through confession man becomes speech even in the face of his own absurdity, suffering, and anguish." So when a woman can confess the truth and name her family's problem as her husband's alcoholism and her own co-dependence, for example, healing can begin. The family system can free itself from what's been likened to an invisible elephant standing in the middle of the living room.

A similar process of "disidentification" occurs with people who may have felt anxious, self-blaming, and hopeless for years—suddenly, they realize that these familiar thought patterns and feelings are symptoms of depression. Only after the problem is named can they find the right treatment and develop the vision for what it would take to become free.

In my organization development practice, I'm called in to companies who need help naming their problems and finding their vision. The first thing I do is to interview the people who work there. The interviews follow a predictable pattern: The first third of the time is spent with the interviewee venting frustrations and perhaps anger. The turnaround comes when I ask them to share their vision, through questions such as, "How could things be different around here?" or "What's the real potential you see?" Almost invariably, what pours out are enormously creative ideas and a pent-up generosity of spirit. Abraham Maslow recognized that we don't simply repress our lower nature, as Freud suggested, we also repress our higher nature. He called this "the repression of nobility."

David Cooperrider, a professor at Case Western Reserve University, developed a practice for people in corporations and other groups to reclaim nobility and find vision en masse. It's a form of discernment called *appreciative inquiry,* in which the focus is placed upon whatever seed of goodness makes life, in that situation, worth living.

Bernadette Cozart focused on the living earth buried beneath the refuse of the vacant lots in Harlem and the hope people gain when they touch the earth. By focusing on something that's already present, even if it's only a whisper, and truly appreciating its potential, vision begins to speak to us. This germ of life is always what we seek in the process of discernment. What's truly enlivening that we can nurture and help to grow?

· ● ·

Reader's Reflection

Think of a situation close to home that's been bothering you. If that situation were to change to what it could be, and perhaps ideally should be, how would it be different? What's the real potential you can envision? Is there one step in your power that you could take toward making that vision a reality?

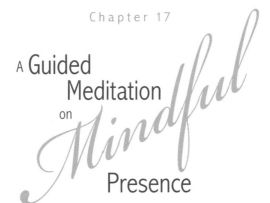

A Guided Meditation on *Mindful* Presence

The meditation that ends this book requires 20 minutes of uninterrupted time in which you can relax and devote yourself to becoming present. If there are other people in your home, it's a good idea to let them know that you'll be unavailable during this time, and turning off the telephone is also a helpful preliminary. If you're a beginner to meditation, we suggest that you use this practice once or twice daily, six days a week. Taking a Sabbath is a good thing, even from a meditation practice. And try it out for a month before you evaluate how it's affecting you.

Meditation requires the skill of concentration that develops over time, so be gentle with yourself when your mind wanders. Just notice when you're no longer present, and bring your mind back to focus. There's a time-honored meditation instruction that compares the mind to a strong bull: It will go crazy if you lock it in a small paddock, but if you turn it out into a big pasture, it will naturally quiet down.

The big pasture is an attitude of mindful curiosity. In other words, it doesn't matter what happens next in meditation—one thing is as good as another. Tension or peace, joy or sorrow, boredom or excitement are all the same: They aren't inherently good or bad; they're just what's happening in the moment. Wait for a minute, or even for a few seconds, and something else will happen. Thoughts are as impermanent as clouds.

You can notice your changing thoughts and feelings with the open curiosity of a child: "Hey, there's peace," or "Oh, here comes anger." Without judgment, thoughts are less sticky. You can relax and notice how they float through the clear blue sky of your natural mind. The sky is spacious—it doesn't try to hold on to the clouds. And even if a storm cloud passes through, the sky in which it floats remains peaceful. That's the attitude of spaciousness: the big pasture. Meditation is about making the shift from identifying with the changing clouds to resting in the spacious sky out of which they come and into which they fade away again. The sky is pure Being, the experience of Now. When you're there, you're present and in your center.

With time, spaciousness carries over into everyday life. You get glimpses of your center, the natural mind, the state of presence, more often. Instead of seeing the world through a veil of thoughts, you perceive it directly, face to face. In those precious moments of Now, your whole self becomes a big, generous Thank You to the universe for all the gifts of life. Those spontaneous glimpses of Being are what motivate us to continue meditation, or to pick up the practice again if we've let it go for a while.

We invite you to try a little experiment. Let your body relax, and focus on something that you've seen before, like your telephone. Spend a little while actually looking at it, seeing the details of it mindfully, just as it is. Chances are that you'll notice things about it that you haven't seen before. Labels fix our experience so that we don't see with fresh eyes. Rather than seeing things, we experience our thoughts about things, and the immediacy of experience fades. When you're mindful, labels fall away, and you open yourself to a world of continually unfolding delight.

The following is a transcription of the meditation on the enclosed CD:

Begin by loosening any tight clothing. If you're sitting in a chair, place both feet on the floor. If you're sitting on a cushion on the floor, make sure that your legs are in a comfortable position that will support you effortlessly for the 20 minutes of practice. This is called your *asana*, or seat, and the more stable your body feels in it, the more effortlessly your mind will come back home to itself. Your back is straight to ensure easy breathing, and your hands rest lightly in your lap, palms up, the dominant hand lightly cupping your other hand. This is called the *cosmic mudra*.

Imagine that an invisible thread is attached to the center of your head, suspending your body like a puppet. Let yourself hang effortlessly from the string. Your head is straight and centered over your body. Your spine is erect, but relaxed. Your shoulders can soften and find their natural balance. . . . Now let your eyelids relax. You may either want to close your eyes or let them relax gently at half-mast. . . . Now notice the surface that supports you, and its pressure against your body . . . what sensations are arising? Can you feel the energy that comes up from the earth? It doesn't matter whether you do or not, just be curious and open to whatever you notice about the flow of life-force energy within you and around you. . . .

Now move your attention to your *hara,* the spiritual and physical center located in the center of your body, about two inches below the navel. Breathe through your nose (unless you're congested), letting the in-breath move down into your hara and expand your belly. When you breathe out, the belly flattens. In, the belly expands. Out, the belly flattens. Focus your concentration by counting now. . . . Breathe into the hara, feel the energy of breath as belly expands—ten. Breathe out of the hara, belly contracts—ten. Breathe in nine and out nine. Keep counting back, one digit for each complete cycle of breath. . . . If your mind wanders, just bring it back to wherever you think you left off.

Can you notice the incoming and outgoing breath as energy? Just be curious about the nature of your experience: What do you notice about the breath that's breathing you? What can you sense in your body as it interacts with the breath? Body and air, body and air breathing, two become one. Notice their union . . . no body, no breath. Just the union of breathing. . . .

Can you hear any sounds? What does it feel like in your body when sound comes in? Focus on the union of sound entering and body receiving. No separate sound, no ears to hear, just the pure sensation of sound . . . energy . . . energy moving and changing.

If you start to think, notice your thoughts entering like clouds passing though the clear blue sky of your spacious mind. Focus on the union between the thoughts and who thinks. What is the pure sensation of thought? Not the words or the content, the sensation itself: the place where thoughts and thinker touch? . . .

Sense yourself. Focus on the union of the energy as what you experience as *your* mind and body touches the energy all around you. No separate body, no separate mind, no separate self—just energy at peace with itself . . . just energy knowing itself . . . just love and intimacy with all that is. . . .

Return to your breath now, moving in and out of your hara. Rest there. . . . Anytime during the day that you need to center, return to the hara and take ten focusing breaths, and then sense yourself. Whatever you feel is the truth of what's unfolding here-and-now. It's the presence of the Holy One. . . .

Our time for meditation is done now. Take a moment and sense how you feel. It doesn't matter whether you're peaceful or restless, content or perplexed. The only thing that does matter is the quality of your attention, and your willingness to stay with your own experience. . . . When you feel ready, come back to the room and open your eyes. . . . Congratulations for taking the time to meditate. As you practice, you'll develop new eyes that perceive everything as part of you, and you as part of everything. Life is precious. Enjoy the gift.

Afterword

Remembering the Essential Wisdoms

We hope that your time with this book has been, and will continue to be, a fruitful exploration of what it means to say yes to change. Continuing the practices of inquiry and meditation that we've explored together will help support your journey home to the wise, compassionate essence that is your true nature. We hope that the brief reminders of essential wisdom on the following pages will stimulate you to keep moving forward through the unknown to the promise of transformation.

The Wisdom of Impermanence

To every thing there is a season, and a time to every
    purpose under the heaven:
a time to be born, and a time to die; a time to
    plant, and a time to pluck up that which is planted;
a time to kill, and a time to heal; a time to break
    down, and a time to build up;
a time to weep, and a time to laugh; a time to
    mourn, and a time to dance;
a time to cast away stones, and a time to gather
    stones together; a time to embrace, and a time
    to refrain from embracing;
a time to get, and a time to lose; a time to keep,
    and a time to cast away;
a time to rend, and a time to sew; a time to keep
    silence, and a time to speak;
a time to love, and a time to hate; a time of war,
    and a time of peace.

Ecclesiastes 3:2–3:8
(King James Edition)

The Wisdom of Initiation

There are three parts to an initiatory rite of passage: separation from the old life; a transitional or liminal stage between what is "no longer" and what is "not yet"; and a return to the community transformed, having discovered one's unique gifts. Offering those gifts back to the community, in service of life, is the capstone of the return process. When change seems frightening, remember that it's the mother of new life, the one story line that we can count on to bring us home to our essential nature and our interconnectedness with the wholeness of life.

The Wisdom of Pain and Loss

The pain and loss associated with change results in the temporary loss of our habitual identity, or false self. The false self is an idealized image of who we are, adopted in childhood to ease the fear associated with possible rejection and lack of love. When this ego self shatters during intense periods of change, a period of great opportunity opens up. It's easier to become vulnerable and real, which can lead to a taste of true nature. When loss makes it clear that the false self can't make us happy, but that our true nature is always accessible, motivation to work toward self-realization increases. This is one of the most precious gifts of change.

The Wisdom of Transition

The time between "no longer" and "not yet" is pregnant with both danger and opportunity. It's truly sacred space. During the initiatory rite of change, the shell of the old life is cracked, and a space of infinite possibilities opens up before us. The chaos inherent in this unknown part of the journey encourages nonlinear events to occur. Synchronicities and unexpected allies are likely to come forth, encouraging healing and transformation in unusual and unexpected ways. When synchronicities occur, or strange events manifest themselves, be on the alert for Coyote Wisdom. What have you been blind to that you can now see? What have you been resisting through the unconscious mechanism of labeling?

The Wisdom of True Nature

You have a true nature, or essence, that's connected to universal consciousness, the Holy One that is always and forever present in all things. Since consciousness (God, Divine Presence, the Source of Being) is always present and available—as St. Paul put it, "closer than hands and feet"—the journey back home to this unitive state of being is instantaneous. The instant in which unity is revealed is always the same: now. Being in the now requires curiosity, a willingness to pay attention to your experience moment-by-moment as it unfolds, without judgment and without any attempt to alter it. This is the path to realizing your true nature or Divine essence.

The Wisdom of Self-Reflection

There are three faces of wisdom: the intellectual ability to tolerate paradox and hold a perspective that's large enough to contain both joy and sorrow; the emotional intelligence to honor all your feelings as messengers of your true nature; and the wisdom of self-reflection that allows you to learn from experience. Self-reflection is the most important type of wisdom because it encourages growth in the other two. We hope that you'll continue to reflect on the questions for inquiry that end each chapter, and revisit them from time to time, not only by yourself, but also with friends who can make the journey so much more insightful and delightful. Friends can often see patterns that you can't see yourself, and their counsel and care can be a great boon to the process of awakening.

Acknowledgments

JB: A book is a living thing, drawing vitality from the insights and writings of many other people. I want to honor the work of all those cited in the text and take responsibility for the way that I've contextualized and interpreted their wisdom. Any mistakes are much more likely mine, rather than theirs.

There are many other people who aren't mentioned specifically in the book but whose work has affected me deeply. Particular thanks go to Sharon Salzberg for her insights on faith, Jon Kabat-Zinn for 30 years of teaching mindfulness, and Oriah Mountain Dreamer for her poetic wisdom and love. I also want to honor the insights of people I've met along the way whose stories have touched me. In order to protect their privacy, I've either changed the situation, gender, time, and circumstances so markedly that they couldn't possibly be recognized; or more commonly, invented a fictional story true to the heart of what they taught me, but not to any set of factual occurrences.

My particular thanks go to my dearest friend and colleague, Janet Quinn, whose facility both for understanding the liminal stage of the change process and for getting me through it following several crises greatly enriched my wisdom. She's famous for popularizing anthropologist Victor Turner's term for the transition period as "the time between 'no longer' and 'not yet.'" To date, three songwriters have picked up on the phrase after Janet and I had given workshops together. Liminal songs about crossing into the unknown are a whole genre of music in themselves, but these three owe their existence to Janet.

I originally heard a much longer and more eloquent version of the brief parable in the Preface from wise woman and storyteller Eve Ilsen, to whom I'm so grateful for her wonderful teaching, singing, and presence. A special thanks goes to Jim Curtan for his insights on chronos and kairos in the movie *Cast Away*.

Finally, I want to thank my husband and co-author, Gordon Dveirin. When I was a mean, tactless editor, he was kind. When I broke down and lost it altogether, he let me cry. When I wanted to ditch the whole idea of coming to an "authentic we" and rewrite his chapters in a way that turned him into me, he held his ground and spoke his truth. That was worth everything, both to this book and to our marriage.

GD: Let me first acknowledge and thank my wife, Joan, who as any discerning reader will see is far more than the principle author of this book. She's also its muse and inspiration. What guides her to say yes, time and again, to a life of tirelessly serving others is a heart that knows no bounds and a joy that knows how to wisely reach through others' pain, as well as her own to bring light where it's most needed. It's been *my* joy to accompany her on this leg of our journey, which now includes you, the reader, whom we most want to acknowledge.

By simply picking up this little book, whatever other benefit you may derive from reading it or doing its reflective exercises, you've already said the most beautiful and self-fulfilling word you can say to life, to the others you care most about, and to the angel of presence that's your own true nature seeking permission to shine through you in every challenging circumstance. Of course that ultimate, relational word is *yes*.

I also want to thank my spiritual teachers, without presuming to have adequately represented the depth of what they've taught me. I include Hameed Ali, whose counsel to "let your mother die," and whose great teaching about how to hold lightly, have been so extraordinarily freeing. Thanks also to my friend John Davis, whose own wisdom about rites of passage he so generously shared; and those, like the nun of grace, whose stories I've alluded to briefly in what I've written.

"**We**": Writing a book is a consuming process. This one took three times longer than we'd allotted for it, necessitating significant accommodations on the part of others. We'd particularly like to thank Luzie Mason and Kathleen Gilgannon, who shouldered a lot of extra work, kept the world at bay, and offered their kindness and support. Chris Hibbard made delicious casseroles that nourished us physically and were also food for the heart. Sara Davidson, spectacular writer that she is, encouraged us and offered support at every juncture. And without Reid Tracy at Hay House, this book wouldn't exist at all. Thank you, Reid, for the trust you placed in us. To our editors, Jill Kramer and Shannon Littrell, and the entire Hay House team—the art department, publicity folks, and the road warriors in sales—you do a wonderful job spreading wisdom that makes the world a better place.

About the Authors

Joan Borysenko, Ph.D., is trained as a medical scientist and is also a licensed psychologist. She received her doctorate from Harvard Medical School, where she also completed three postdoctoral fellowships. She is the co-founder and former director of the mind/body clinical programs at the Beth Israel Deaconess Medical Center in Boston and a former instructor in medicine at Harvard Medical School. A pioneer in integrative medicine, Joan's work encompasses creativity, women's issues, relationship-centered healing, spirituality, and the inter-religious dialogue. The author of 12 books and numerous audiocassette programs, she also writes a monthly column, "Staying Centered," which appears in *Prevention* magazine. Her Website is **www.joanborysenko.com.** You can reach her office at (303) 440-8460.

Gordon Dveirin, Ed.D., is president of Dveirin and Associates, a consulting firm in human and organization development. The focus of his work, with clients ranging from private-sector businesses to the Smithsonian Institution, is on facilitating conscious collaboration. Gordon's spiritual development has been guided by two decades of practice as a student of the Diamond Approach to self-realization as taught by A. H. Almaas. He's currently the strategic architect of The Nurturing Pedagogy Project, a three-year national demonstration and research project that's addressing the social, emotional, and spiritual needs of public school students as an integral part of their education. He's also the designer and facilitator of the Fully Human Leadership Program of the Women's Vision Foundation. You can reach his office at (303) 459-0522.

The authors, who are husband and wife, are co-founders of the Claritas Institute for Interspiritual Inquiry, which offers a two-year certificate program in interspiritual mentoring. Spiritual mentoring, as practiced in established wisdom traditions where it may be referred to as *spiritual direction* or *spiritual guidance,* involves skillfully assisting the spiritual formation of another by facilitating the following three movements:

1.   **Alignment:** Personally connecting to the Source or Ground of Being.

2.   **Discernment:** Distinguishing between genuine guidance arising from that deep connection and conditioned reflexes of the ego.

3.   **Action:** Acting in the world with the spontaneity, grace, and compassionate wisdom that comes from authentic inner guidance.

Mentoring is a process of Presence and companioning that helps the other to connect to his or her own inner guidance. The ideal result for those assisted is a life energetically lived as engaged spirituality and passionate growth toward wholeness. Such a life invites a harmonious state in which the mind, heart, and hand work together to create a better world for the individual seeking spiritual direction, and for all beings. If you're interested in the program, please contact **Kathleen@ClaritasInstitute.com.**

Hay House Titles of Related Interest

The Amazing Power of Deliberate Intent,
by Esther and Jerry Hicks (The Teachings of Abraham)

Eliminating Stress, Finding Inner Peace (book-with-CD),
by Brian L. Weiss, M.D.

The End of Karma, by Dharma Singh Khalsa, M.D.

Getting in the Gap (book-with-CD), by Dr. Wayne W. Dyer

Mending the Past and Healing the Future with Soul Retrieval,
by Alberto Villoldo, Ph.D.

Power Animals (book-with-CD), by Steven Farmer, Ph.D.

Practical Praying (book-with-CD), by John Edward

Silent Power (book-with-CD), by Stuart Wilde

Spirit-Centered Relationships (book-with-CD),
by Gay and Kathlyn Hendricks

Spiritual Cinema, by Stephen Simon and Gay Hendricks

The Wise and Witty Stress Solution Kit, by Loretta LaRoche

All of the above are available at your local bookstore,
or may be ordered by visiting:

Hay House USA: **www.hayhouse.com**
Hay House Australia: **www.hayhouse.com.au**
Hay House UK: **www.hayhouse.co.uk**
Hay House South Africa: **orders@psdprom.co.za**

• ● ● ● •

We hope you enjoyed this Hay House book.
If you'd like to receive a free catalog featuring additional
Hay House books and products, or if you'd like information about the
Hay Foundation, please contact:

Hay House, Inc.
P.O. Box 5100
Carlsbad, CA 92018-5100

(760) 431-7695 or **(800) 654-5126**
(760) 431-6948 (fax) or **(800) 650-5115 (fax)**
www.hayhouse.com

Published and distributed in Australia by: Hay House Australia Pty. Ltd. • 18/36 Ralph St. •
Alexandria NSW 2015 • Phone: 612-9669-4299 • Fax: 612-9669-4144 • www.hayhouse.com.au

Published and distributed in the United Kingdom by: Hay House UK, Ltd. •
Unit 62, Canalot Studios • 222 Kensal Rd., London W10 5BN • Phone: 44-20-8962-1230 •
Fax: 44-20-8962-1239 • www.hayhouse.co.uk

Published and distributed in the Republic of South Africa by: Hay House SA (Pty), Ltd., P.O. Box
990, Witkoppen 2068 • Phone/Fax: 27-11-706-6612 • orders@psdprom.co.za

Distributed in Canada by: Raincoast • 9050 Shaughnessy St., Vancouver, B.C. V6P 6E5 •
Phone: (604) 323-7100 • Fax: (604) 323-2600

Tune in to **www.hayhouseradio.com**™ for the best in inspirational talk radio featuring top Hay House authors!
And, sign up via the Hay House USA Website to receive the Hay House online newsletter and stay informed
about what's going on with your favorite authors. You'll receive bimonthly announcements about: Discounts and Offers,
Special Events, Product Highlights, Free Excerpts, Giveaways, and more!
www.hayhouse.com